Invisible
Imprints

A Memoir by

MARY D'AGOSTINO

ISBN: 0692178775
ISBN-13: 9780692178775

Cover and interior by Publish Pros
www.publishpros.com

For Papa

Contents

Introduction

First, I must confess to you, the reader, that it was never my intention to write this book. It was originally my intention to write another book, which I believed deserved far more recognition than the one you now hold in your hands. Yet, whenever I made an attempt, with pen in hand, nothing happened. I remained frozen, staring at a blank page for endless hours while another story demanded instead to have a voice, where the words flowed easily as if they had a life of their own. A story constructed of words from a child I thought had long since been silenced.

Memories cascaded one by one onto the pages with details that captured my whole attention. I surrendered. Gradually the story revealed its own merit, which I'd questioned up to that point. What value could a story that happened so long ago have? Moreover, who would care?

Still, I allowed memories to unfold without resistance as they revealed the mind, heart and spirit of this child who lived for a very long time in an unusual place with nuns who often provided unusual experiences.

As most parents, teachers and health care providers might agree, it's doubtful we will ever really know or understand childhood. Much of what we already know has likely come from second-hand observational data, as opposed to what is actually happening within the mind and heart of a small child. Are children really so resilient? How does a very young child actually process being stripped of love and belonging? What power of reasoning might they summon to survive such an event? On the following pages, I've opened a small window through which the reader can glimpse, and perhaps find some of these answers and a hint about an ending I never saw coming.

During my own education in psychology, it never occurred to me I held a story that could shed some light on how a young mind perceives and translates the circumstances of her environment to secure both her own survival and spirit — that is, until I began to write. There is much to be learned from children, who far too often are silenced before they can reveal the accurate knowledge and observations they've discerned about the adults around them.

Yes, there will be parts of this story that may touch your heart. It is my hope there will also be other lovely times when it tickles your heart and lifts your spirit. In the end, I almost feel like this book tried to write itself — all it needed was for me to just simply — open the door.

MARY D'AGOSTINO

Separation

Though earth and man were gone,
And suns and universes cease to be,
And thou wert left alone,
Every existence would exist in Thee.

EMILY BRONTË

Childhood, home of our earliest memories, those silent companions to each soul. They come suddenly, uninvited, like a cat pouncing on your lap and circling into its curves, determined to stay a while. They invade thoughts and even rule actions. Then, they color and shape who we become and survive those dramatic events that should have pushed them aside forever — loves, births, triumphs, deaths and betrayals. And still they linger, hovering on the back shelves of consciousness for all the days of our lives, waiting…why?

Looking back, her eyes held more than tears on that early spring day in the 1940s as she looked vacantly off into space. Her eyes held *resolve*. The train sped along to a destination unknown only to me. There was no reaching my mother with my pleadings not to have to leave home again. Promises to be the goodest little girl in the whole, whole, world, and to always obey and eat everything on my plate just melted into the clacking sounds of steel wheels meeting steel tracks. The apple-cheeked conductor moved slowly down the aisle as he punched tickets, his glasses perched precariously on the tip of his nose. When he reached us and saw my despair, he glanced at my mother.

"Oh my goodness, what could possibly be sooo terrible to cause all these tears?"

She looked past him and gave a helpless shrug. He moved on. In an effort to quiet my sobs, she made a promise that day.

"Even if you're not all well in two months, I promise I'll take you home anyway, just like the last time you went away, remember?

Anyway, a simple enough word. A free, almost carefree word that conjured up all kinds of thoughts. It meant I belonged to her, regardless of whatever might be wrong with me; certainly, enough to be reclaimed, fought for even. It confirmed I had roots in a family that nothing could break, not even the illness that silently lived inside me. It meant acceptance just as I was.

Anyway. How could one word be powerful enough to allow for the first full breath since leaving our house that morning? A deep, full breath, not the little gasps of air sucked in through sobs. It seemed to revive every part of a body that felt it was dying. Because, to a child, fearing abandonment by her mother is equivalent to death itself. The word "anyway" that day was truly the most beautiful word in the whole English language, but not quite beautiful enough to erase the terror still engulfing me. Oh yes, of course I believed her, after all she was my mother and I was six years old, powerless and voiceless.

The yellow cab traveled a long way after we left the railroad station. The landscape outside moved rapidly toward a destination so foreign to me it was as if I were being drawn into the orbit of another planet. So many trees, most of them bare, some with just a hint of pale green haze to signal spring was not far away. We traveled miles before even a house dotted the landscape here and there. Every turn of the cab's wheels took me further and further from our three-room flat over a grocery store in the Bushwick section of Brooklyn, the only place on earth I wanted to be that day.

Finally, the cab slowed along a high, black iron fence with an impressive opening. As it turned onto an interior road, I heard what would become a very familiar sound, the crunching of pebbles beneath the wheels. I clutched my mother's hand as she paid the driver, as if nothing on earth could ever separate us, then we both hesitantly got out of the cab, sinking deep into the thick white layer of those smooth pebbles. Outside the cab there was something different in the air, a fragrance I'd never experienced in the city, the scent was so distinct it seemed to even have color. Green — deep, deep green, like the freshly washed spinach my mother prepared at home. As I looked around, I had the distinct feeling of being placed in the center of a living, breathing and growing world.

A red brick building sat among four smaller buildings, forming almost a circle. In the middle of the circle stood a very tall, beautiful bronze statue of Jesus with outstretched arms. Upon entering the larger building, a nun greeted us with a warm, practiced smile from the above landing. She descended the steps and extended her hand to my mother and said to me, still smiling, "Well now, you must be Mary D'Agostino."

I recall wondering, How could she already know my whole name? Did she know we were coming? Was this already planned and decided? Sometimes six-year olds have difficulty with the obvious, especially when they're in deep distress.

The nun was not very young or pretty, yet her appearance somehow managed to stay with me. She displayed an expression of composed calm, but that would very soon change. The glasses she wore were almost rimless, giving her a look of indisputable authority. Her hands were thin, with skin so pale they appeared translucent, especially over her knuckles and the joints of her fingers. Her habit was white with a headpiece I had never seen before. The veil covered a solid piece across her forehead about an inch-and-a-half wide, highlighting the rest of the white habit in a rather dramatic way. Large, black rosary beads hung from the side of her waist. Flowing down beneath the bib were panels both in front and back of the dress, with a cross in the center of her chest. Her title, suitable enough, was "Mother Superior."

The nun ushered us into her office and seated herself at her desk in front of a window while motioning for my mother to take the chair opposite her. She pointed to a second chair for me on the side of her desk. Refusing it, I continued to clutch my mother's hand while sitting on her lap. The two women chatted about the trip while the nun scanned through a file — my file. The tension in the room hung heavy, palpable actually, when I heard a faint knock at the door. A small boy, perhaps a year or two older than me, entered the room and with a very soft voice, asked if he could pick a book from the book-case. The nun beamed at the boy and told him he could pick any book he liked.

Suddenly, she stood up and asked my moth-er to step outside with her for a moment. I jumped to my feet to join them. With exquisite calmness, the nun assured me my mother wasn't going anywhere, and for extra emphasis asked her to please place her purse on the desk.

"Now, would your Mother ever leave without her purse?" she asked.

Of course, that was very unlikely, so I sat down again, satisfied they would both return in a few moments. I watched the boy at the book-case, totally engrossed in picking and choosing from a number of shelves. I wondered if he actu-ally read the books or just looked at the pictures like I did. After several interminable minutes, I slid off the chair, went to the door and started to open it. The nun sharply slammed it shut. It was then I knew it was all over — my mother would never return to that room with me. I felt savagely betrayed.

We often speak about the extraordinary physical strength displayed by ordinary people when confronted with a life-or-death situation. This is no less true of children, as I demonstrated that day with my approximately forty-pound body. I stood in front of the door, placing my right hand firmly around the knob and my left hand tightly around my right hand. I braced my left foot firmly against the door molding. Slowly and with every ounce of strength in my body, I pulled against the strength of the nun. The skin of my right palm burned, almost tearing from the friction against the knob, yet the pain seemed to belong to someone else, because my hand felt only superhuman strength. Slowly the knob turned. Then, while simultaneously straightening my left leg, I pulled with almost herculean strength, and the door actually started to open. First a crack, then almost enough for my hand to fit through.

I heard the nun cry out, "Sweet Mother of Jesus!"

I continued to inch my fingers along the edge of the door, fully prepared to let her chop them off if she regained control of the door. How could the pain be any worse than what I was already feeling? Instead, the nun pushed her whole arm through the opening and wrestled my fingers from the knob as she shoved my body backwards. I fell to the floor and gave out the only thing left in me to give, screams that seemed to leave the earth and penetrate the universe. Primal screams, for certain, that echoed out far beyond the room and brick building to those who would remember them for a very long time to come.

Suddenly, the door flung open and in the midst of unimaginable despair, I was engulfed in the arms of the woman who would become my surrogate mother. The shock of her passionate hug and stroking, along with her proclamations of my great beauty, froze the moment. Her words then turned to elaborate promises for so much fun and happiness in my new home, and she somehow managed to subdue my screams to just suffocating guttural sobs. No one in my life, other than my own mother and other female members of my family, ever expressed that kind of passionate affection to me. The folds of her habit wrapped around me, making it almost impossible to breathe. The cloth felt rough against my skin and smelled fresh and clean like the bed sheets at home. With one arm around my shoulders and her other hand tightly holding mine, she whisked me out of the room while the boy at the bookcase stood frozen in sheer horror.

The nun moved me along a hallway, up some stairs, then down others, opening some doors and closing others. She led me through what appeared to be an underground passage with sand piled high on both sides, followed by a narrow corridor with a laboratory on each side. Two women in white coats looked up from their microscopes when they heard us passing through. They smiled and tilted their heads lovingly at me. By then my legs had become incredibly weak, making it impossible to keep up with the nun's pace. She had to half drag me at times. All the while she talked non-stop, calling me her "beautiful new baby chick" and reminding me again and again how much I was going to love being at All Saints Hospital. Finally, we stood in front of a closed door and she announced we arrived.

It was a small sunny room with a single bed against the right wall and a white metal cabinet next to the bed. There were two windows in the room, each facing a different view. One of the windows looked out on the rear grounds of the building, where three see-saws stood snuggled in the same white pebbles we walked on in the parking lot. Sun streamed in through the other window, which faced another building connecting it to the one I was in by a narrow red brick bridge. The second door in the room led to a spotless full bathroom. On the floor sat a large doll almost the size of myself, and next to the doll was a nice carriage, but far too small to accommodate the doll. I turned to the nun to ask who the toys belonged to and saw her face for the first time.

She was an older woman, thin and sturdy, with a pocked complexion and angular features. Her name was Sister Martha. Her habit was different from the one Mother Superior wore, it was plainer, just the usual veil with the wimple wrapped closely around her forehead and face. The fabric of the entire dress was coarse with no tailoring at all. Sister continued to make real attempts to quiet my wailing while she wiped away my tears. Yet, I couldn't reach her when I begged to just be able to say good-bye to my mother. Anything more was quite surrendered by then, the inevitable was well at hand.

Even a child knows what goes against the natural order of things, and being expected to remain in a strange place with total strangers without some form of closure with my own mother certainly qualified as going against the natural order of things. Grown-ups, I thought, would simply never do something like that, it would be too cruel to imagine, especially for nuns. Didn't they work for God?

Before I could ask about the doll and carriage, Sister Martha removed my coat and hat, placed them on the bed, and told me she couldn't remain with me much longer because she had to check on the other children in the building, who I would soon be joining. I begged her to please not leave me, but again she insisted she had to, reminding me how the other children would be wondering where she had gone and might become frightened.

"Now, you wouldn't want that to happen, would you?"

Before I could answer, she was out the door and I heard the faint click of the lock. I rushed to one of the windows, not even realizing I was in an entirely different building from the one I had entered earlier with my mother. I'd been brought clear over to the other side of the grounds and was facing a building next to the one we had entered. I stood there, determined to wait for her to emerge. No matter how my legs ached and trembled, there was no way I could leave my post. I waited for what seemed like hours. And it was.

Finally, I heard a key turn in the lock and Sister came bouncing into the room looking very cheerful. She became a bit annoyed, however, when she noticed I was still crying so hard and said sternly, "Now stop this crying and come away from that window!"

Did she really believe I could just transfer my attention to her and forget my own mother? I tried to explain to her that I needed to stay at the window so my mother would see me when she came to say good-bye. She looked startled by my reply and told me my mother had left hours ago and was most likely back home again by then. Left? The word pierced my stomach with the force of a dull blade, making it very hard to breathe.

"NOOOO! that's not true! my mommy would never just leave me here without even saying good-bye, I have to say good-bye to my mommy, I HAVE TO!!"

The panic was unimaginable — it hemorrhaged from every part of my being, spilling out at the feet of a strange woman I meant nothing to. My life and the world as I knew it had ceased to exist. My mother would never have left that day without at least saying good-bye. That is, if she had been allowed to. Yet, it would take more than half a century before I would discover she had collapsed outside the nun's office that day. Had I known, it might have made a huge difference in the rest of her life, and mine.

The nun looked at me long and steady through her non-descript dark hazel eyes apparently only meant to see out of, but not for anyone to see into.

"This is your home now Mary. You'll be very happy here with all the other children, you'll see. Just stop this crying. I'll be back with your food tray as soon as I can."

She appeared quite serious. To her, the matter was settled. Your mother has gone, returned home by now, and this will be your new home from now on. For her that was the end of it, clearly implying there must be something wrong with me for not making the instant adjustment. Again, the sharp click of the lock behind her.

My mother had left, and with her gone, I was left in a vacuum of nothingness. My legs caved and I slid down to the floor powerless, feeling the vague sensation of evaporating into the air of the room. The only place to turn was inside myself where I could find both the comfort of my memories and the magic of imagination.

❦

"Come now Mary, I want you to finish everything on this tray so you'll get well real soon."

Her voice jarred me from another time and place — our kitchen at home where I would have been sitting at the table waiting for my sister to come home, and the three of us would have dinner. I was remembering how I'd usually push my food around on my plate until my mother, out of habit, would start to feed me, never pausing whatever conversation she and my sister were engaged in. How I loved listening to them talk, especially when they weren't arguing. They had so many opinions about everybody and everything, they could go on for hours. Listening to them sometimes prompted me to question where I stood in their whole scheme of life.

Ours was a broken home. My father hadn't lived with us for as long as I was alive. I was, by a wide margin, the youngest of four children. Paul, the oldest by fifteen years, was red-haired and freckle-faced, a serious and unhappy young man who took things too hard. He had a stomach ulcer by age sixteen and would later learn he was ineligible for military service, so he attended St. John's University and lived in my father's apartment. Tony, my second older brother, was almost the exact opposite — athletic, quick to smile and always making jokes and eating peanut butter sandwiches. Those sandwiches were perhaps our only bond since I also loved them, and he rarely paid much attention to me otherwise. Tony was in the army and my mother said my father was also. That left Josie, my 16-year-old sister, who saw herself as my mother's right arm and the surrogate mother of the family. I was her personal toy and she loved to fuss over me, constantly changing my hairstyle to resemble whatever little girl she saw on her way home from school that day. I felt desolate on those rare evenings when she went to a movie with her friends, regardless of how much they bribed me beforehand. God, how I adored my sister. To live in a world without her was unimaginable. She was my world.

So, the two of us lived with our mother in a small three-room flat over a corner grocery store in Brooklyn. I knew we were poor because my mother worked, and no one else's mother worked outside the home in those days. Her job was very important to her, even if it was in a "sweat shop," as they were called then. My mother was proud of the fact she was the only sample maker of the silk lampshades made in the shop, and she knew the owner held her in very high esteem. I recalled what a nightmare it was when she couldn't leave for work because I was too sick and there would be no one home to take care of me. And, of course, I was sick all the time, making me wish I was grown up already, so no one would have to take care of me again.

But, I wasn't grown up, and on some days, total strangers took care of me. After Mass one Sunday my mother went over to the rectory and talked to a priest. He listened intently to her situation and give her the name of a lady in the parish who needed to make some extra money and was willing to take care of me while she worked. The first morning it was so cold and windy outside that walking to this woman's house seemed to drain all the energy out of my body. It was early when we arrived, and she was busy at the stove, preparing pancakes for her children who weren't even up yet. After being assured I would be fine, my mother kissed me good-bye and left.

The woman's kitchen felt warm and cozy as I watched her make breakfast. One by one her children appeared, all sleepy- eyed and groggy as they sat down at the kitchen table. I envied the fact they could take for granted their comfort and sense of belonging. There were three of them, all older than me.

The oldest was a teenage boy, who, when he saw me asked his mother, "Who's the kid, Ma?"

The two younger children were still too cranky to give anything more than a scowling side glance.

"Oh, Father Murphy gave her mother my name because she has to work and needs someone to take care of her daughter. Wouldn't you like a pancake too, honey?"

I shook my head. Nausea had already started to creep up my throat. Her relief at my answer was unmistakable, confirming how little I mattered in that kitchen. The woman's hands darted back and forth from stove to table as she served her brood's demands for more pancakes, syrup or juice, while her mouth fired away questions at them.

"Do you have your milk money? And what about you? Did you do your homework? Do you have the note I wrote to your teacher?"

I watched them all like an observer peering in their window. I didn't belong there. I was the outsider.

"Why don't you at least unbutton your coat, dear," the mother suggested when she finally noticed me again.

You see, for a child, there is nothing worse than being left completely in the care of strangers. They feel instinctively that they don't matter as much as children who are cared for by their own mothers. Little could I have known on that cold winter morning just how soon I'd be taken from home, and for how long I would be in the care of yet another stranger.

When my attention finally returned to the room after Sister left, I stared at the food on the tray for a very long time, wondering if I had somehow caused myself to be in this place because I was such a poor eater and gave my mother such a hard time. If only I had forced myself to eat more maybe I wouldn't have been so sick and could be home with my family where I belonged. I concluded my present situation was all my fault. For certain there would be no giving this strange woman a hard time. I picked up the fork and with supreme effort forced myself to eat, dreading the taste of everything on the tray, especially those wretched prunes for dessert. But I needn't have dreaded it, because it all tasted the same — salty, like tears.

Children's voices got closer and closer until they seemed to be coming from the other side of the wall. The sound of their soft animated laughter made me feel less alone as night fell. The door opened abruptly and there she was again, veil all puffed up with air about her shoulders, making her look more like a large, white bird landing in my room than a nun. She carried a folded brown shopping bag and what appeared to be night clothes. She glanced briefly at the tray but said nothing. Instant relief.

"I have a surprise for you, Mary."

When I asked her what it was she replied simply, "You'll see."

With that, she went into the bathroom and soaked and rung out what looked like long strips of rags about an inch and a half wide and placed them on the nightstand while she untied my pigtails. She parted my hair into sections and asked me to hold one end of the wet strip on top of my head as she very deftly circled the hair around the strip, all the while proclaiming how beautiful I was going to look the following day. When she finished, I had six or seven sopping wet banana-shaped things hanging around my head, which I was expected to sleep with. I was certain this alone would be grounds for my mother to remove me from this place as soon as I could inform her of this practice. She was always fanatical about keeping my long hair as dry as possible so I wouldn't catch cold, or worse. I'll be home long before the two-month promise she made, I mused to myself.

Sister opened the brown paper shopping bag, which had my first and last name written on it in bold letters. She picked up my pale green coat still lying on the bed where she had left it, turned it inside out, folding one shoulder into the other, and placed it down neatly into the shopping bag, along with my matching bonnet. She told me to remove my clothes, and the same exactitude was applied to my heavy sweater and the rest of the outfit I wore that day, leaving me with a distinct feeling of gradually disappearing into the shopping bag.

When my clothes were gone, she asked me to step into a one-piece gaily printed pajama with a flap in back.

"I'm not a baby anymore!" I protested.

She laughed out loud for the first time, making her face appear softer, but no less homely. She explained how she simply couldn't find a two-piece pajama small enough to fit me, but promised if I ate real well, she would consider big-girl pajamas the next time. Having said that, she tucked me affectionately into bed, picked up the shopping bag containing more of me than was left behind, turned off the light and left.

Lying in the darkness, I tried very hard not to move too much so as not to notice how foreign everything touching my body felt. When I thought of my mother and sister, I was sure they were probably still sobbing over me as I was over them, but even that thought brought no comfort. They had each other, what could possibly be better than that?

Feeling more exhausted than ever before in my life, I slid as close to the wall as possible, knowing at least that there were children on the other side. The plaster wall felt so cold and smooth against my cheek that was hot and stinging from so many hours of crying. The haunting sound of a distant train whistle reminded me of the events of the day and just how far I really was from home. The room itself held a total stillness I never before experienced, broken only by the night noises outside from hooting owls and creeping ground critters. No honking cars, no people chatting on street corners, no clacking of ladies' heels on the sidewalks. It was all too much to take in. After a very long time something wonderful and unexpected happened — I fell asleep.

We open our eyes slowly following a nightmare, never sure if the horror of it is still with us or not. When I opened mine the next morning the reality of the day before lay neatly all around me. It had all really happened. I rolled to the opposite side of the bed and noticed my shoes placed side by side on the floor. I was overwhelmed by a feeling of actual love for them. They were mine, the only connection I had to everything I left, or had taken away from me. The laces must have still had the invisible traces of my mother's fingers, and I wanted to kiss them and cradle them in my arms. But just as I reached down for them, Sister burst into the room with a cheery "good morning!" She held out a thermometer for me to place under my tongue and at the same time took my pulse, writing the results in a black and white notebook.

I studied her face closely as she went about these movements, hoping perhaps she might look more familiar and less homely than the night before. She looked neither. She struck me as a woman who knew she wasn't attractive, was it the way she moved, perhaps? She wore her habit as though it were the only real identity she had, something to keep herself well hidden. Sister reached for the rag curls on my head and was delighted that they were completely dry, just as she had predicted. I was pretty shocked myself. Again, she reminded me how pretty I would look when she removed them. But first there was breakfast, which she would bring to me as soon as she had the girls settled down in the dining room. After she left, I slipped out of bed and went straight to the windows. No sign of life or movement anywhere, just trees, trees, and more trees.

When Sister returned, she carried both a tray of food and clothes for my first day in my new home. Breakfast consisted of my least favorite food in the whole world — hot cereal. She placed the tray at the foot of the bed with a reminder to finish everything. I ate standing, even though a chair had been provided, and focused on what my hair might look like after she removed those rags. It was my way of helping myself get the hot cereal down. Flushing it down the toilet required a lot more courage than I possessed that morning.

When Sister returned again, I was given my first lesson in making up a bed, something every girl was expected to do, and do perfectly. Having never made up a bed before, I was fascinated by the exactness with which her hands went about it and was determined to do it perfect on my first try, especially those hospital corners. I wanted very much to please this woman. Children know instinctively when their survival is at stake, or when they think it is, and I was sure mine was. Sister Martha removed my pajama and dressed me in a rather nice outfit, nicer in fact than the one I had arrived in. Next, she untied the top of each rag, allowing long, tight curls to cascade down over my shoulders. When all the curls were unrolled, she scooped up a bunch of hair on top of my head, and wrapped a lovely silk ribbon around it. She stood back, eyed me with approval, and for a brief moment, I felt special to her.

After she left, I walked around the room, vaguely amused by the sensation of the curls bouncing around my head. If only my mother and sister could see me, they would be so shocked at how different I must look without pigtails. But the amusement was short lived, and

I was once again plunged into loneliness and fear, wondering how much longer would I be kept alone in that room. I was certain it would only be a little while longer.

The hours dragged on, the big doll sitting upright on the floor mocking me with its red smile and two big white teeth. There was no desire to play with anything in that room except the rubber door stopper I discovered behind the bathroom door. It could be clamped on to any flat surface and would make a loud popping noise when I pulled it off, providing the only sound to break the silence. My family once again flashed across my thoughts and I realized there was no one in my present environment who I loved, or who loved me. I had a mother, two brothers and a sister who I loved intensely and who I belonged to. Yet there I sat, in the middle of a room, completely alone. Me and a rubber door stopper. How was it possible?

At noon Sister returned with a dinner tray. Lunch was called dinner and dinner was called supper, she explained. I had a list of questions for her.

"When can I see my mommy? How long will I be in this room? When can I go home?"

Sister Martha answered none of my questions as she floated around in her dismissing manner, talking at me about the rules of the hospital (she called it the sanatorium), which centered for the most part around the obedience of the children. It was clear that being obedient was hugely important, but what I couldn't know then was just *how* important.

After dinner, she put the tray aside and drew the shades, rolled back the bedspread, told me to undress down to my underwear and get back into bed for an afternoon nap, where I should remain until she returned. I could hear the girls in the next room returning from the dining room and settling down for their naps too. Napping was not something I was very successful at even at home, so it was no surprise that I couldn't come close to falling asleep. I just laid there wondering what my mother and sister were doing at that exact moment and feeling very confident they were doing nothing but thinking about me. I had to believe I was still important somewhere. They couldn't possibly be going on with life as usual, could they?

After a very long time, I heard stirrings behind the wall as if the girls were getting up from their naps. Then Sister burst into the room (she never walked through the door) with a thermometer in one hand, her black and white notebook in the other, just as she had done in the morning. I realized this was yet another one of the daily rituals. She took my pulse again and made no comment when she noticed I had been crying instead of sleeping. It was then I decided to never let her see I had been crying again, better to wait until after she turned off the light at night. Only then could I allow the watershed of tears to convulse my body until I could hardly breathe, then fall into the deep, deep, dreamless sleep reserved for very young children.

"How many other children are in this building with me, Sister?" I managed to find the courage to ask.

She told me there were twenty-four other girls living at St. Michael's. I was amazed, but at the same time somewhat relieved, since whatever was wrong with my heart must also be wrong with theirs. Somehow, that realization allowed me to feel less damaged. Sister then snapped up the shades and told me to look out the window after she left because she would be taking the girls for a walk and I could see all of them for myself.

"Now, won't that be nice Mary? Wouldn't you like that?"

I dressed quickly, stationed myself at the window and waited. Soon the building became very still, I could see small girls with the nun descending the stairs. I watched as she instructed them to assemble just below my window. They waved wildly, some even jumped up and down as Sister remained behind them, smiling broadly. There were so many of them, and they all appeared to be so happy. How could this be possible? There was simply no way to wrap my mind around such an absurdity. After a few minutes, the nun said something to them and they quickly organized themselves and waved good-bye. I watched until they were completely out of sight. Everything became very still again. I wondered if I had been left alone in the building. The possibility was more than likely.

When they returned, I heard the children in the adjacent playroom. Their laughter provided such a contrast to the silence of my room, I wished it would go on forever. Before long it was supper time and once again everything was hushed. When Sister entered with my tray, I was almost delighted to see the dessert was applesauce instead of those wretched prunes. It was far too early in my experience at the hospital to know prunes one night and applesauce the next would be another ritual that would never be broken for the remainder of my time in that place. And, after only one day, it felt as if a month had already passed.

The following day started exactly as the first. However, when Sister opened my door mid-morning she was accompanied by a male doctor. When I saw him I backed away, crying.

"Do you want me to hold her down doctor? This one is a real screamer."

Screamer? Was she talking about me? What happened to her "beautiful new baby chick." Now she wanted to hold me down like I was some kind of wild animal? I felt once again betrayed and painfully aware this woman was not someone I could trust — not ever. The doctor was much annoyed by her question and waved her off dismissively. I liked him immediately.

Dr. Tara was a stocky man with thinning hair, soft brown eyes and a calm, open face. He sat down slowly in the only chair in the room as if he suddenly remembered he was very, very, tired and held out his hand with a promise not to do anything to hurt me. He even offered to let me hold his new fountain pen while he listened intently to my heart.

When he removed his stethoscope I immediately asked, "Can I go home now? Can I?"

He took in a long, deep breath as he stroked my head lovingly with his meaty hand. Then he asked me to promise to listen to everything Sister told me to do while he motioned for her to dress me. Sister Martha almost flew across the room in obedience and dressed me in total distraction. I sensed her energy change while in his presence, as if she were experiencing the pure joy of finally being able to actually snatch a moment of his attention all for herself. It is nothing short of remarkable how much children are aware of, even at such a tender age. Before I realized it, they were both out the door with the familiar click of the lock.

Several more days went by in my isolation room filled only with coloring books, cutout dolls, quick cheery visits from Sister and unseen hours of endless crying. Toward the end of the week, Sister started to question me about where I went to school and if I knew any prayers. I told her I had gone to Catholic school when I wasn't sick in bed and I knew the Our Father and Hail Mary. This information seemed to please her and she promised that evening after supper she would come for me, so I could stand in back of the playroom with her as the children said the Rosary. And she did come for me that evening, just as she had promised. The two of us stood in the back of the playroom while she listened intently to my prayers. It was amusing to see how hard it was for the children to refrain from taking a sneak peek at the new girl from the isolation room as they sat cross-legged on the floor facing the front of the room saying the Rosary. They made a stunning scene for me to observe.

Before tucking me in that night, Sister told me I would be receiving my First Holy Communion very soon, even though I was only six and not seven, which was the standard requirement. I asked why.

"Just in case something should happen, you'll go straight to heaven, Mary."

I wondered where I would be sent if something should happen to me before receiving my First Holy Communion, but I thought it best not to ask. Sister and I had a clear conflict of interest on this issue, since she was showing me the surest way to heaven and I only wanted to know the surest way out of there and back home. Besides, she needed to teach me the Act of Contrition for my first confession before a time could be set. When she finished informing me of this news, there was only one pressing question to ask.

"Will I be seeing my mommy on my special day, Sister?"

"But of course you will, Mary."
Then it would be a very special day indeed.

House Rules

Those things which hurt, instruct.

BENJAMIN FRANKLIN

There were more tests and exams, but the big day finally arrived, when I was considered medically safe enough to join my twenty-four sisters. After nap time one afternoon I left that lonely room. Sister and I walked to the playroom where the children were already gathered. Sister opened the door and did what would become a very familiar gesture, she tapped the glass on the upper portion of the door several times with the gold band she wore on her right ring finger. The taps resulted in instant silence and attention. The girls stared at me with intense curiosity as Sister introduced me.

"Girls this is Mary D'Agostino, I want you all to be very friendly to her and help her learn the rules here at St. Michael's."

The sea of faces slowly parted, allowing me to enter both their play space and their lives.

The playroom was a large, sunny room with several windows along one side, an upright piano against the front wall and a console radio in the corner. Several bookcases filled with games, puzzles and books stood between the windows. There were wooden straight-backed chairs against any remaining wall space, and on a table was a pretty doll house. The floors were the same shiny, dark-brown, marbled asphalt tile that covered every floor in the building. Other than a crucifix over the door, I can't recall any other wall ornament, except perhaps a picture of an angel with great white wings looking over the shoulders of a small boy and girl at play.

The girls gathered around me, each announcing her name and asking me questions about where I lived. How old was I? What was the isolation room like? Was I scared? It was hard to know who to answer first. When I told them I was six years old they were quick to inform me that made me the baby of the building. Then I admitted to being really scared in the isolation room. But, what surprised me most, was learning none of them had experienced it since the they had all come to St. Michael's from the hospital building or another hospital where they had been bedridden. Then it was my turn to ask questions, but I had only one.

"When do we get to see our parents?"

"Oh, visiting day is one Sunday a month," they echoed.

I gasped in spite of myself. They were so matter of fact about it I was sure I must have misunderstood. But no, they all reassured me once a month was the rule. And they seemed to be fine with that. Was I missing something? Didn't they care? Had they all just forgotten their families and accepted this place as their real home? Of course, that could never be true, yet it begged the answer to my next question, the one I wished I'd never asked. "How long have you girls been here?"

"Two years," said one girl.

"Oh, I'm here almost three years," said another.

I was stunned, unable to speak, hardly able to even breathe. The ceiling started moving sideways in a funny way, so I leaned against the piano stool. First, I struggled with trying to breathe, then with the overwhelming feeling of pity for those poor children who were so sick they had to remain in a hospital for so long. At the same time, I frantically searched my mind for a thought that would rescue me from believing I could have a similar fate. Then I remembered. The promise! I decided it would be best not to tell my new sisters I would only be with them for the next two months. Only then did I take in a long deep full breath and allow my very soul to leap in giddy relief.

For the remaining playtime that day it was impossible to fit in, no matter how hard the girls tried to engage me in their fun and games. Everyone wanted to be my best friend at once, while I just wanted to observe them and sort out for myself how I might survive in this foreign environment. The fact these girls were all older and bigger than me didn't help. I was not at all happy about being the baby of the building; I just wanted to go home and continue being the baby of my real family.

At suppertime Sister Martha appeared at the door, tapped the glass for attention and told us to line up. I scurried in obedience just as the other girls did, and we all marched down the hall in silence. The dining room was another bright room with windows along one side and five round tables neatly set. I was assigned a table and instructed to sit there for every meal until I was told otherwise. We all sat down almost simultaneously. It was so nice to at least have company to eat with. Sister disappeared into the kitchen behind swinging doors and emerged minutes later with a tray of dishes of food she placed in front of each child. No one picked up their fork, so neither did I as I watched each child be served. Sister stood in front of the room made the sign of the cross and everyone said grace.

"Bless us, our Lord, for these, Thy gifts, which we are about to receive from Thy bounty through Christ our Lord, Amen."

Everyone picked up their forks and began to eat. I was amazed to see the children dig in and actually appear to enjoy their food while I just slid the food around, hoping it might some-how disappear into the plate. I said nothing during the meal as the children animatedly talk-ed about things I knew nothing about. I was far from knowing their world. When the children's voices rose above a certain level, Sister Martha emerged from her kitchen and without uttering a word, pulled gently on a string attached to a small bell placed on the front wall. Like magic, all their voices dropped down to a hushed hum. When it was time for dessert, out came those wretched prunes again, with no objections from anyone. After being allowed more chatting time, we lined up for our trip to the dorms as I wondered what kind of experience awaited me there.

Our building had two dorms, the first adjacent to the playroom, the second at the other end of the hall adjacent to our classroom. I was as-signed the first dorm near the playroom. Each dorm had either twelve or thirteen girls with six beds against one wall and the rest across the aisle against the windows looking out onto the play area and fields of vegetables in the background. The beds were typical white-framed hospital beds, separated by white metal cabinets for each child's personal belongings. The bedspreads were all identical, white-on-white stripes, covering two pillows on each bed. Aside from a teddy bear or doll on several beds, the room was void of any color. On the front wall hung a wooden crucifix.

The dorms were very busy places before bedtime, and the girls all knew exactly what to do. I had been assigned the bed nearest the entrance. Since I had no personal belongings to put in my cabinet or to share with the rest of them, I just sat on the edge of my bed and looked on. They talked happily, compared their little treasures, negotiated important trades, told secrets and just enjoyed each other's company. Then without being told, they each folded down their bedspreads and started to undress, neatly folding each article of clothing they removed before putting on their pajamas. I closely followed every move they made, but since I didn't have pajamas, I waited in my underwear for Sister to return.

Before very long Sister was hurrying down the hall with my pajama in hand. When I unfolded it, she was quick to see my disappointment since again it was another one-piece pajama. Just as I feared they might, the girls all giggled when they saw me in it, especially since the buttons holding up the back flap were missing, and I had to hold it up with one hand. But I wasn't especially upset by their amusement at my expense, because they were so sweet and gentle about it, like I was their baby sister, and I had nothing to fear from them.

The last evening ritual was the enormous task of rolling up the hair of almost every girl in those rag strips, a task Sister did completely alone. Each girl knew the routine well, as she patiently stood in line with comb and wet rags near the doorway where Sister waited. Sister proceeded to part, section and roll up each one's hair and hand back their combs and ribbons to be worn the next day. I watched with fascination, while waiting my turn. When it came, Sister reminded me my hair was longer than any of the other children's, and she hoped on visiting day my mother would give her permission to cut it so it would be easier for her to roll. I felt like I had been stripped of everything, now she wanted to cut off my hair too?

After everyone's curls were rolled up Sister announced it was time for lights out. The girls dashed about, retrieving their belongings from one another and putting them into their own cabinets. Since no one said otherwise, I assumed lights out didn't necessarily mean silence as well. I was wrong.

The dead silence in the dorm after the nun clicked off the lights unnerved me. I felt again the familiar longing to be home with my mother and sister. If I talked to the girl in the next bed, she might head off the flow of tears welling up. After all, I reasoned, she must surely feel the same way I did, if I could only hear her feelings about us being in this place it would help so much.

I whispered, "Are you going to sleep?"

"No, why? What's the matter?"

"I miss my mother so much, I just want to go home."

"Yeah, I know, I miss home too."

Before I could ask another question, the light clicked on, and Sister was standing over me.

"What is going on here?"

The girl volunteered instantly, "She's crying because she misses her mother and wants to go home, Sister."

The nun's face was livid with rage as she proceeded to tell me how selfish I was, thinking only of myself. How I didn't care that I was upsetting the other children who also missed their families and wanted to go home too. With this, she grabbed one of the pillows from beneath my head and slammed it down over my face, shouting, "Now go to sleep!"

I heard the click of the light switch but couldn't be sure if she had left the room or not. I lay there utterly stunned, terrified as to what might happen next. I dared not remove the pillow pressing down on my face for fear she would put me back in that isolated room, or maybe something even worse. There was simply no way to predict this woman's actions. My mind couldn't comprehend such a violent act for such a small infraction. *What kind of a place did Mommy leave me in?*

Sweat started to break out on my face, I knew I had to at least move to get some air. I turned my head slowly to one side, and with my index finger made a small opening between the two pillows to let some air in. My mother and sister flashed across my mind, but I couldn't allow myself to even think about them. That night there was something I needed even more than wanting to be back home with them — I needed to breathe.

∽∾

The bright light was blinding, and the air felt icy on my sweaty face as the nun removed the pillow from my head the next morning. Her face reflected sheer horror.

"Why didn't you take that pillow off your face?" she gasped.

"Because you put it there."

She made no reply, but about-faced, went straight to her little cart parked at the foot of my bed and removed one of the thermometers from its alcohol-filled vial. She walked back to me and placed it under my tongue. It was then I noticed her hand was shaking, badly.

After she finished her temperature ritual, she left the dorm without another word. I marveled how everyone got washed, dressed, made up their beds, untied their rags, and with combs in hand, lined up for Sister's return to comb each girl's hair out and tie a ribbon on top of her head. It was like observing the inner workings and movements of a finely tuned instrument, all I had to do was somehow fit in without getting too badly clobbered. Since I had absolutely no idea how to negotiate my environment, I wondered how would I ever manage to accomplish this.

As we all lined up to go down the hall for breakfast, I prayed, "Please God, at least let this day start with cold flakes, not hot cereal."

My prayer was answered, and after breakfast we lined up again for our walk down the hall to the classroom. There was a lot of lining up, like we were all linked together for the duration, without a chance for individual movement of any kind, something like being in prison.

I was relieved to see the teacher was not a nun, but a regular lady who looked like she could be anybody's mommy. She wore lipstick, smelled like perfume and smiled a lot too, especially when Sister introduced me. Her name was Mrs. Hurst. And, while I can't honestly say I recall learning a whole lot about the three R's in her room, I do recall experiencing some rather special moments there, which I shall get to later.

The midday meal always consisted of meat, potatoes and vegetables, followed by milk and dessert. Afterward, we would march back to the dorms and undress down to our underwear, while Sister drew all the shades for our afternoon nap. No one dared talk during those nap times, which I thought would have been rather nice to do since I never ever came even close to falling asleep. But surprisingly, the children were quite content to snuggle in and one by one drift off into predictable slumber.

After what seemed like hours, Sister returned with her cart of thermometers, snapped up the shades, took each child's temperature and pulse, and recorded them in her black and white notebook. Then she would rush off to do the same in the second dorm while we dressed, made up our beds and waited in line for our trip to the playroom, where we stayed until suppertime. This routine would not change during my confinement. Yet strangely enough, it provided perhaps the only thing resembling both comfort and stability in a place that I felt sure would never hold joy.

Once joined with the other children, learning the Act of Contrition for my first confession was simple. The girls would let me repeat it over and over again until I could recite it without a hitch. Then they patiently explained what to expect when I entered the confessional room, which was Sister's small office, and what to say first after kneeling down. The words "Bless me Father, for I have sinned," were a bit confusing, since I couldn't figure out what sin I might have committed, but that would soon change.

Sister seemed genuinely happy when she talked about my upcoming special day. She told me the little boy who would be my partner for his First Communion in church was working very hard at learning his prayers as well. She had also chosen a very beautiful white dress and veil she was certain I would love. I looked forward to the big day too, but for more than receiving my First Communion. What I was really looking forward to was seeing my mother and maybe my sister. I wondered if that might qualify as a sin and if I should confess it to the priest during my first confession, which was coming up on the following Saturday. At least then I would have something to confess, a fact that was becoming more and more worrisome to me.

The Saturday I was to meet Father Fitzgerald for my first confession was soon upon me. I needn't have been anxious about it, because Father Fitzgerald struck me as the kindest-looking man on earth — short and round with wavy light brown hair that fell into little ringlets around his cherub-like face. But it was his eyes that really impressed me. I can still see them to this day. Father's eyes were deep blue, and they twinkled and smiled even when he didn't. He sat in a chair in front of Sister's desk in her small office, a small confessional kneeling bench had been placed for me alongside his chair.

When I walked into the office he smiled, before bowing his head as I shyly knelt down.

"Bless me Father for I have sinned. This is my first confession and these are my sins, but I'm really sorry."

I told him first off that I had talked once after lights out, but left out the part when Sister had almost suffocated me to death as a result. Then I confessed to not finishing everything on my plate at mealtimes, while my mind searched frantically to come up with something really interesting. Not being able to come up with anything, I launched in earnest into my perfectly rehearsed Act of Contrition. I watched him closely, holding his brow as if he were actually interested. Was that a smile I detected beneath his little nose? Of course it was, I was certain of it. At the end, he asked me in his thick Irish brogue to say three Hail Marys and three Our Fathers for my penance, while simultaneously blessing me. As I stood up to leave, I felt one huge step closer to receiving both Jesus and my mother.

The playroom was a quiet place on those Saturday afternoons after confessions had been heard. Each girl found a place to pray her penance prayers before we all went into supper. On that particular Saturday, Sister had promised she and I would go over to the chapel afterwards, so I could practice for the next day's ceremony with my partner. However, the plans had been changed, she said, because the boy was not ready for his First Communion. I wouldn't be going down the aisle with him at the chapel as initially planned, but would receive my communion in the hospital building where I had first been admitted. This news made me a bit anxious as to what that experience might be like. But, as long as it didn't interfere with my mother's visit, I felt little else. Why would I?

III

Touched By Angels

Nothing in all creation is
so like God as stillness.

MEISTER ECKHART

In those days, receiving communion required fasting after midnight the night before, which meant there would be no breakfast served until we all returned from Mass. Sister came in that morning with her temperature cart as usual, and as she took my pulse, told me she would soon be bringing in my Communion outfit. I was starting to feel the excitement of the approaching event and anticipating what my mother and maybe even my sister would think when they saw me all dressed up. The other children got dressed and made up their beds while Sister dressed me in my white clothes. She seemed very pleased when she finished, and even presented me with a lovely prayer book and rosary of my very own. I wished I could have seen for myself what I looked like, but there weren't any mirrors in our building. Sister said Mother Superior would be coming by shortly to take me to the hospital building for the ceremony. I hoped when I got there I wouldn't have to see the room where I had last seen my mother.

When Mother Superior arrived, she was full of smiles and compliments on my appearance as she took my hand and we both left for the short trip to the hospital building, using the outside route instead of the underground passageway. The air smelled so clean and fresh at that early time of day, I had almost forgotten how wonderful it was just to be outdoors in the morning. It was also the first time I had seen Mother Superior since our struggle in her office.

As we walked in silence, she must have been thinking the same thing, because she stopped and quietly reminded me, "Mary, do you remember how hard you cried when you came to us several weeks ago?"

How could she even imagine I would forget?

"Well, on the day you leave us to go home, you'll cry just as hard, I can promise you that."

Her words were so ludicrous I didn't even attempt to reply. I fell silent and half skipped alongside her, trying to keep up the rest of the way. Yet, in my mind that morning, there was no doubt the hand I was holding on that brief trip, belonged to a madwoman.

When we entered the building, I recognized the landing over the stairway. My chest felt tight as we walked down the familiar corridor, only this time Mother Superior would stop to give me specific instructions. Before doing that, she went into a room and returned with a tall, thick white candle, beautifully decorated in gold, tied with a lovely white taffeta ribbon and handed it to me. The streamers were long and fell far past the hem of my dress. Mother then lit the candle when she saw Father Fitzgerald arrive. He was in full Mass vestments, with a white brocade shawl wrapped around his shoulders and covering the chalice he held close to his breast. With bowed head, he took his place behind me.

"Now Mary, you will follow me slowly down this corridor, and Father Fitzgerald will follow you. Do you understand?"

"Yes Mother."

We were both whispering. Slowly, the three of us walked to a room at the end of the hall, and entered a scene I was not prepared to witness; nor did I realize it was only steps away from my experiencing sacredness.

As I stepped through the entrance of the room, the whiteness of everything in it and the bright sunlight streaming through the windows made it close to blinding. Then my eyes fell upon the children. There were four of them, two on each side of the room who were propped up high against the pillows of their beds completely dressed in white Communion clothes, right down to their stockings and shoes. Their veils gently cascaded over their shoulders and pillows, making them look incredibly angelic. Between each pair of children stood a nun in attendance.

Slowly, I followed Mother Superior as we passed between their beds on each side of the room to a small altar, where a kneeler and seat had been placed to the side just for me. Mother motioned for me to stand beside the bench as Father walked up to the altar, placed the chalice and genuflected before it. I stood there in a trance as I tried to take in both the extraordinary beauty and sadness of the scene. The room was very still. Lovely bouquets of flowers lay at the foot of each girl's bed. Blood-red roses, soft pink carnations and bright yellow daises created a stabbing contrast against the stark whiteness covering everyone and everything else in the room. I wondered where such beautiful flowers might have come from. Beside two of the children's beds stood tall green tanks with round dials and knobs on their top. These tanks held oxygen, but I didn't know that at the time. Plastic tents over the top portion of the children's beds had been temporarily folded back. I realized very quickly these girls were gravely ill, but my young mind was simply not equipped to take that reality in.

Father said Mass in Latin, while Mother Superior sat behind him to one side and I sat on the other. I held my hands upright and tightly pressed them together with my thumbs crossed, just as Sister Martha had instructed me to do.

But I prayed in a way that was mine and mine alone.

The gentle ringing of bells told me Communion would soon follow. When it was time, Father lifted the chalice from the altar and turned to Mother Superior, who held a gold plate in both her hands. The two of them turned and walked slowly toward the first child, who had already been lifted ever so gently from the pillow by the nun. The girl weakly extended her tongue to receive the sacred Host over the gold plate Mother held under her chin, then closed her eyes as the nun again placed her ever so gently back down on the pillow. She appeared only half awake for the remainder of Mass. Father gave Communion to the two nuns and remaining children before turning in my direction. I felt my heart pounding harder than I ever remembered as I received the Host and tried to contain the feelings exploding inside me. When Mass was over, I stood up to receive the candle Mother held out to me. Once again, I followed her out of the place I believed, with the certainty only very young children possess, to be one of holiest places on earth.

In the corridor afterwards, Mother took the candle from my hands, blew out the flame and went to her office to get her camera to take my picture in front of the statue of Jesus. Outside, while she tried to focus my image in the camera, she repeatedly asked me to open my eyes and smile, but the sun was so bright it was impossible to keep my eyes open, and even more impossible to mask my smile after what I had just witnessed. We walked back together in silence to the small chapel where another Mass was getting underway. The crunching sound of pebbles underfoot and the chirping of birds overhead were the only sounds breaking the serene stillness of the morning.

Once inside the chapel, Mother ushered me to a pew in the rear of the church where the older girls from another building were already seated. As I knelt beside her my thoughts began to replay the scene in the hospital room. Before I could contain them, sobs convulsed my body, breaking the promise I had made to myself in the isolation room. The girls around me stared with sympathy and confusion on their faces, not understanding where such intense emotion could possibly be coming from. Mother

Superior, on the other hand, guessed exactly where it was coming from, as she leaned down and whispered in my ear, "Mary, you should be very grateful and thank God you were the only one who was well enough to be out of bed for your First Communion, think about those other poor children."

How I wished I could have screamed, "But I am! I am, you stupid, stupid woman!" I only nodded an affirmative yes.

When the regular Mass ended, Mother Superior returned me all red-eyed back to Sister Martha. They exchanged a knowing glance between them and I joined the children of my home building. Of course, the girls were full of questions.

"Where did you receive Communion? What was it like there? Why couldn't you receive it in the chapel like everybody does?"

A good question, one I was wondering about too, but I hardly made any attempt to answer their questions. My mind was already focused on that afternoon, when I would be allowed to see my mother, despite of the fact it wasn't visiting Sunday. The nuns had made a special allowance for the occasion, and I was very anxious for the appointed hour to arrive.

We ate our Sunday dinner consisting of roast chicken for the main course and ice cream for dessert — another routine we could absolutely rely on to never change before going in for our naps. Finally, I could be alone with my thoughts and feelings of that morning, and daydream about my mother's visit and how she must already be on the train and very close to arriving.

After our usual temperature check, Sister again dressed me in my Communion clothes for the second arrival of the day from Mother Superior, who would accompany me to the auditorium where the parents could join their children. When we arrived, Mother sat me down on one of the metal folding chairs not far from the entrance. I stared at the door as each visitor entered and gave their name to the nun who was greeting them. Suddenly, there they were, both my mother and sister, giving their names to the nun. They had already spotted me as I bounded from my chair and ran to their crushing hugs and kisses. The familiarity of my mother's scent was almost dizzying as she covered my face with kisses until my cheeks hurt. Josie looked on until it was her turn. Then sitting back, they both took a good long hard look at me in my white clothes, marveling at how beautifully I had been dressed for the occasion from veil to shoes, and the excellent quality of each item, not to mention the long, cascading curls replacing the pigtails.

"Tell us, how was the ceremony?"

My chest caved when I realized how much I lacked the words to even try to express the power of what I had witnessed that morning. Instead, I searched for something I could tell them that they could relate to and understand. "The children had beautiful flowers on their beds," I said passively.

My mother gasped at this, because she had wanted to bring me a bouquet of flowers too. However, when she remembered, they were already in the train station where there were no florists available, and it was too late to look for one on the street without missing their train. My sister listened intently to her explanation, and kept nodding her head in agreement. I told them it didn't really matter. And it didn't.

Then my mother reached into her purse for the present she had bought to mark my special day, a lovely white and yellow gold cross necklace. When she clasped the latch, I felt very loved, and a bit grown up too, having never had a real piece of jewelry before in my life. I asked why she left that day without even saying good-by.

"I wanted to, but the nun wouldn't let me. You can't imagine how upset I was." Her face clearly showed how stressful the day had been for her.

Still, I needed to get to my real plea. "Mommy, please, please take me home right now. I hate it here so much I can't wait two whole months, it's just too long, I'll die! Please take me home today. I promise I'll eat everything you give me, I'll be so good you'll never have to yell at me, never ever."

Her expression never changed as I struggled to describe what being in an isolation room was like. I could hear how my words were not coming even close to what I felt, nor what the experience was like, nor, for that matter, what was actually going on inside me. I was too young and lacked the language needed; everything I said sounded like baby talk. My feelings were confirmed as I watched my sister nervously glancing around the auditorium as I spoke, taking in the scene of all the children visiting with their parents, and the nuns as they strolled up and down the aisles.

I thought, she isn't even listening. She just can't wait for this to be over, so she can get out of this place and go home with Mommy again, where it's all safe and the same.

The futility of my pleas gradually began to sink into my being, and I had to content myself with the reminder of the two-month promise my mother again assured me of. I never told her about Sister placing the pillow over my face on my first night in the dorm. Deep inside, a feeling forbade me from revealing something so terrifying. Or perhaps it was even more terrifying to think she might not believe me if I had.

Visiting time was suddenly over, good-bye hugs and kisses were being exchanged all around us. I sobbed on both their shoulders and necks while they struggled to contain whatever feelings they might have been experiencing and gently tore themselves from me, with passionate promises to see me on the next visiting day. Mother Superior appeared from out of nowhere, smiling, as she took my hand and led me away. If she said anything on our way back to St. Michael's, I wouldn't know, my thoughts were still back in the auditorium with my mother and Josie, envying them their freedom to go home together.

They were going back to an uninterrupted life, surrounded by the same people they were born to, eating the same foods they ate all their lives, sleeping in their own beds, smelling the tomato sauce cooking on Sunday mornings, going to church together. These things they could still take for granted. They didn't have to fear anyone, learn to live with them, obey them unconditionally, and eventually surrender to accepting them in order to survive. My family hadn't the slightest clue of how frightening my life had become, and realizing this made them seem strangely innocent and naive. Suddenly, I felt very old.

The children were in the playroom when we got back. Mother Superior turned me over to Sister Martha without a word. Sister noticed the cross hanging from my neck and admired it as she led me into the playroom. The girls said I was lucky because I had been given an extra visiting time while they still had to wait for regular visiting Sunday. Lucky? What silliness, I thought. I went through the motions, joining them in whatever activity was already underway, until we heard tapping on the upper glass portion of the door and Sister telling us to line up for the walk down the hall to the dining room for supper.

I stood out among them that evening in my white communion dress as my special day rapidly drew to an end. But I couldn't manage to connect with anything like feeling special. I wondered how my family might have celebrated the occasion, surely there would have been a special cake with lots of icing. There would have been presents from my grandmother, and my aunt and uncle who would have come over to our house with my two younger cousins. Timmy, their oldest, was only three years younger than me, and more like my little brother, since his mother took care of me during those years more than my own mother did. And there was their new baby, Jeana, who I hadn't even seen yet. But I wasn't part of their world any longer. In my world, I could only hope we wouldn't have prunes for dessert on that particular evening. But we did.

The days following my Communion consisted mostly of observing the routine and the girls who had it down pat. At the center of that routine of course, was Sister Martha who called all the shots. She seemed to care for us exclusively. If there were any other people helping her, they would have been very much in the background, since we saw only her. Pleasing her to not incur her wrath seemed the central point of our existence. From morning temperature checks to lights out, virtually nothing changed from day to day.

Occasionally, Mother Superior would drop by with a group of women whom she referred to as "our visitors." They were very well dressed, furs and all, they smiled a lot and were quite impressed when we all curtsied with the precise timing of a chorus line as we greeted them on cue, "Good morning (or afternoon), ladies." Sister always appeared so pleased at such times and full of pride, both for our good manners and appearance. And well she should have, since it took great pains to keep us looking well.

It was a huge job every evening to roll up all those wet rag strips for almost every one of her twenty-five chickens, as she loved to refer to us, and keep those curls tied up in satin ribbons. As for manners? Well, our only choice was absolute perfection.

Mealtimes, as I said, were very predictable. Thursday was my favorite meal day of the week. That was the day we had cold suppers of sandwiches, with fresh fruit for dessert. My favorite sandwich was of course peanut butter and jelly, not only because I loved them, but because it made me feel at home since my brother Tony loved them too and paid the most attention to me when we shared them. Afterward, Sister would pull out large canisters filled with candy, just like I remembered seeing in candy stores back home, and place them on a stand in front of the dining room wall under the silence bell. We would get in line and buy candy with whatever pennies we had, feeling like we were actually choosing and purchasing candy from a real candy store. Sister would put the candy in tiny brown paper bags, so each girl could carry her sweet treasures to the dorm to be eaten later or traded away. I wasn't much of a candy lover. I enjoyed giving away most of what I bought, then watching the girls as they devoured the contents of one wrapper after another.

☜☞

The days were warming up quickly, which meant more time spent outdoors. Now I could take part in those walks I had only been allowed to observe from the isolation room window. The paths we walked along had lovely grottoes, where Sister would encourage us to take a few minutes to kneel at the foot of the Virgin Mary statue and pray.

My prayer was always the same, "Please Blessed Mother make my mommy take me home."

I'd stare into her stone eyes until my own eyes hurt, hoping she might give me a sign my prayers were indeed heard, like they were for the saints in the stories Sister told. Sometimes, I even caught Sister watching me during those prayerful times. I wondered what she was thinking, and how much she already knew about my future in that place.

The paths were becoming more and more beautiful, as rows upon rows of apple blossoms came into bloom, along with pink and white dogwoods. Their beauty took my breath away. As a child from a large city, I had never seen anything to match the beauty all around me. I soon developed a real appreciation for the colors of all growing things and the smell of freshly mowed grass. At times, the sound of the breeze rustling through the canopy of trees we played beneath was so calming and soothing I'd walk away from my sisters to quietly enjoy the swooshing sound of the leaves. I was discovering the beauty of nature could fill the emptiness inside me more than anything else at that point in time. And I was learning to use the skill well.

Me near the statue of Jesus

IV

Prayers and Promises

I will never leave you comfortless:
I will come to you.

JOHN 14:KJV

During the days and weeks following my
First Holy Communion, not an hour
passed when I didn't think of home and
my family. I counted the days until I would leave
All Saints Hospital and join them as promised.
Sister would get very annoyed at times, because
I questioned her constantly about how many
weeks had passed since I had first been admitted. As for my hospital sisters, I went through the
motions of being a part of their lives, but I re-

mained remote. My body may have lived among them, but my heart and soul were still at home, and the time for leaving these girls drew closer and closer. In my estimation, there was only one more visiting day before the two-month promise would be fulfilled, and that thought alone sustained me in my daily life.

I was learning very young that an individual can endure almost anything if they know it's only for a definitive amount of time. Therefore, forming strong bonds with the children was simply unnecessary. In the meantime, the routine of the days was becoming more and more a part of my consciousness, providing predictability and comfort in knowing what to expect next, an element non-existent in my own home. If there is one single thing children thrive on, it's predictability, and our days certainly provided that.

There were other rituals introduced during those early days too, like all of us going over to the hospital building about once a month to be examined by Dr. Tara. He would sit in front of the fluoroscope screen and observe the white peppermint substance, which was spoon-fed to us by one of the Mothers. He closely observed the substance as it slid down through each esophagus, past each heart. As we stood in the doorway of the room, waiting our turn, I always wondered what determined whose heart was healthier than the others, since everyone's looked exactly the same to me. Afterward, we'd go into a second examining room where we were weighed, and a female doctor with a strong European accent examined us without ever saying a single word, or even cracking a smile. Her remarks were only directed to the nun in attendance, Mother Katherine, who always looked directly into your eyes as if she knew something very special about you. The lady doctor had short jet-black hair and eyebrows, sallow skin, and appeared quite angry with the world in general. After she listened to each girl's heart, she would record her findings in a solid black binder with our name on it and place it back on a shelf. She could do all this without ever looking at our faces or saying a single word. I determined we must have been faceless statistics to her, and I disliked her intensely.

In between class time, naps and playtime, Sister would often fill the gaps with storytelling, especially on rainy days when we couldn't go outdoors. The children relished in her stories that always seemed to surround visions people had had of one sort or another. She talked a lot about guardian angels, how we each had our own who was assigned to us at birth and never left our side. I drew more comfort from this possibility than anything else she told us. I even developed the habit of squeezing myself to one side of my bed at night and at nap times, so my angel could lie down if she ever became weary from standing over me. I also concluded a guardian angel might be a useful ally in helping me to get home. Maybe she could talk to God on my behalf. I decided to pray to her every time she even crossed my mind and I diligently kept that promise.

Most of the girls were Christian, but there were several Jewish girls who would stay in the playroom when Sister was giving religious instruction in the classroom. Sometimes, after her instructions concerning the crucifixion, one of the girls would decide to tell these children that the Jews were responsible for killing Jesus. This would naturally cause them to become very upset and anxious. During those times, Sister would pull them aside and talk to them in her office. I often wondered how she managed to console them because they always returned feeling so much better. One girl was determined to convert to Catholicism and was convinced her family would allow it. However, I don't recall that ever actually materializing.

As my promised departing visiting day approached, living at the hospital had become more bearable because I knew the end was eminent. I certainly cried less, even at night when everyone else in the dorm was fast asleep and no one could hear me. When the usual roast chicken dinner was served that Sunday, I finished everything on my plate, just like the rest of the girls did. Nap time afterwards was filled with anticipation as to how soon my discharge would take place. "Mommy must already be on her way. I bet she's even carrying different clothes for me to wear since the weather is warmer now. I can leave with her today!"

The auditorium was buzzing with excitement, as it usually did on visiting day, all of us squirming on our metal chairs, watching the door for our parents to appear. The first thing I noticed when I saw her was that she didn't seem to be carrying much in her arms. When she slid into our spot, her hugs and kisses were exhilarating as we both tried to talk at the same time. My mother was telling me how wonderful I looked, as I tried to ask if we would both be leaving together that day because her two-month promise was up. But it seemed her first interest was only in getting Sister Martha's attention so she could ask her usual questions: "Does she have any more fevers, Sister? Is she eating?"

Sister gave a reassuring "no" to her first question, and a somewhat encouraging response to her second question: "Well, she is trying to do better."

My mother used these responses in defense of what she then told me. "You see? See how well you're doing? If I take you home now, you'll get sick all over again, so you have to stay here until *they* tell me you're really well enough to come home, Bella Mamma."

She always called me that when she was being particularly loving. Apparently, it's one of
the most endearing names an Italian mother
can call her child. But on that day, her words
had just murdered the only hope I had had to
sustain myself during the last two months. Oh
God! What would I do now?

Scorching hot tears gushed down my face,
burning my cheeks like acid. There were no
words to speak, just disbelieving, choking, guttural sobs. My mother, seeing my despair, started crying too and looked a bit desperate herself, but no less resolved regarding the reality
that had existed for her all along. The rest of
that visit remains a blur to me to this day. Except
for perhaps hearing myself saying over and over
again in my head, "But you said anyway!"

With her promise broken, the only thing
left for me to do was pray. I was determined to
pray to this man called Jesus, who Sister talked
about incessantly. Sister said He performed lots
of miracles. She said He even raised someone
from the dead and made a blind man see again,
so my miracle should be really easy for Him.
I was just a little kid who wanted to go home.
How hard could that be? I also prayed to His

Blessed Mother Mary. I would beg God to show me a way to survive whatever remaining time I had to spend in that place. And He did.

The answer to my prayers came very shortly after that visiting day. One afternoon, while we were in the playroom, came the familiar tapping on the upper glass portion of the playroom door. There stood Sister Martha holding the hand of the cutest little girl. She was tiny, like me, with thick chestnut-brown hair, large brown eyes and an adorable little pug nose. Her name was Alicia, and from the moment we locked eyes, we became best friends. Alicia didn't look particularly frightened that first day I saw her, she looked more curious than anything. She too was six years old, which gave us an instant connection. Her mother was Italian and her father was Irish. She had older brothers, so she was the baby of her family, just as I was.

From the beginning, we did just what new lovers do, we told each other everything about ourselves as fast as we could, each sentence ending with, "Me too! Me too!"

I shared with her the day of my First Communion, and she was very familiar with the scene I described since she had spent twenty-one days in an oxygen tent in the hospital building herself. Her parents were allowed to see her any time, day or night, she said. Alicia told me these things with the same remoteness she displayed all the time. Years later, when we met again, she denied remembering she had ever even been at All Saints Hospital. How interesting. No, I thought, how impossible.

We played almost exclusively with each other, Alicia and I, and going outdoors became an adventure. I had someone to explore with, to discover with and most of all, to laugh with. Together we looked for grasshoppers to chase or caterpillars to put on twigs and watch them dangle back and forth like trapeze artists. The ground held all kinds of creepy crawly things, and we both took delight in chasing all of them. It seemed like my whole world changed. I had a real friend of my very own. I finally felt connected to someone.

One summer day, Sister picked both of us to weed the pansies in the large stone planters just outside our building. After showing us exactly how to do it, she left us outside alone. We were beside ourselves with the joy and freedom being left unattended gave us. It felt like we were outside our own family homes, and we were giddy with excitement.

Suddenly, Alicia blurted out, "Oh Mary, I love you so much!"

I was stunned and embarrassed. As much as I believed my family loved me, I had never heard those words before. Ours, was not an "I love you" family. It was more of an "Eat, eat more!" family. That's how they expressed their love.

She looked at me with beckoning eyes for a reply. My throat felt dry as I pushed out the unfamiliar words, "Uh...yeah, me too, I...I...uh...love you too."

"Let's be friends forever then, okay?"

"Forever? Yes, okay, forever."

God had, indeed, answered at least part of my prayer. He made it possible for me to feel alive again, and I could go more than one whole hour without even thinking about my mother.

Seasons Unfold

*Know that yesterday is but
today's memory and tomorrow
is today's dream.*

KAHLIL GIBRAN

Days melted into weeks, weeks slid into
months, and months quietly succumbed
to the passing of the first year, with all
the inevitable changing seasons. It was perhaps
during the second summer when our routine
was only slightly altered. After supper on warm
evenings, we went outside and lined up in front
of our building, just as everyone from the other
buildings did, forming almost a perfect circle of

children and house mothers. We would pledge allegiance to the flag and sing the "Star-Spangled Banner" to honor our soldiers fighting abroad, followed by the lowering of the flag by one of the mothers. That was about as close as we came to the war raging in Europe and Japan at the time. We knew there was a very evil man in Germany, whose name was Adolph Hitler, who did terrible things of which we knew nothing. We also knew the Japanese had done a really bad thing in a place called Pearl Harbor. Aside from that, and the several servicemen we saw on visiting days, we were kept completely insulated from any knowledge of a war going on in the world around us.

The console radio in our playroom was never turned on, and we were absolutely forbidden to touch it. I longed to hear the sounds of the great bands of the era, Tommy and Jimmy Dorsey, Glenn Miller, Benny Goodman, or Artie Shaw's "In The Mood." Their music was so familiar to me with three teenage siblings around during my preschool years. The voices of the Andrew Sisters were almost a constant background sound in our kitchen, and my sister knew the words by heart to all the songs of the time. Words to "I'll Be Seeing You," "Don't Sit Under the Apple Tree With Anyone Else But Me," "Shoofly Pie and Apple Pan Dowdy," or "You Made Me Love You" would circle around in my head for hours before finally falling asleep at night.

Those summer evenings also provided us with a chance to see the children who occupied the other buildings around us. St. Luke's was the only male building and housed boys ranging in ages only up to ten. They of course, provided us with the most amusement, since the boys couldn't stay still for any length of time, and their house mother (the only nun other than Sister Martha titled Sister) had to reprimand them constantly. I found myself comparing her to our Sister Martha. Sister Emily was short, quite plump, giggled and wore a constant smile. She looked so warm, soft and motherly, while Sister Martha was wiry, stern and in complete control of her brood. I would have given anything if we could have switched house mothers. I was totally convinced the boys had it much easier than we did. They had a house mother who showed love for them in every gesture and accepted the fact they were "just children," while ours demanded obedience. Those evenings also gave us a chance to see for ourselves who the cutest boys were, so we could talk about them and giggle until lights out.

Next came St. Helen's building, where the girls ranged in age from approximately ten to fourteen, followed by the hospital building, then St. Mary's, our nearest neighbor, where the older girls were fifteen to eighteen. Their house mother was Mother Mary Grace, the youngest and prettiest of all the nuns. I envied how the girls could interact with her just as if she were one of them. Those were the girls who also reminded me most of my sister Josie, and I loved to gaze at them in their bobby socks and sweeping pompadours, just like hers. The feelings they evoked were very bittersweet.

During those early summer days, we noticed men were working on something pretty ambitious behind our building, digging and pouring cement into a large square opening. Then one evening Sister announced these men were building a pool just for us. We were ecstatic and bombarded Sister with questions about its completion and how soon could we use it. She told us to ask our parents to buy us a bathing suit on visiting day and bring it the following visiting day. By then the pool would be completed, and the weather warm enough for us to jump in.

I had never been in a pool in my entire life and felt like things were really starting to look up, especially when Sister said I'd been chosen as the official flower girl for the sanatorium and needed to ask my mother to also buy me white shoes. I would be needing a pair of my own, she said, for various occasions, like First Communions and special holy days. Again, the girls called me lucky, and unlike the evening of my own First Communion, I actually felt as if I just might be. I was achieving celebrity status among my peers and was even introduced as the hospital's "official flower girl" to those smiling visiting ladies when they came by with Mother Superior in their fashionable outfits.

On Sunday, my mother was very eager to fill whatever requests I had and was delighted to hear about the pool. While there were still lots of tears on those visiting days, they started to be filled with more and more inquiries about other members of my family. I was most interested in hearing about my little cousin Timmy and whether or not he had forgotten me. My mother was always quick to assure me he asked for me all the time, he couldn't wait for me to get well and come home to play with him again.

In my heart I seriously doubted that, but there was nothing I could do about it. I was resigned. In time, there were fewer things for me to ask about on the home front during her visits, so I just enjoyed the hugs and kisses she showered on me. Sometimes, I even felt sorry for the children around us whose parents seemed to only show them affection upon arriving and leaving, with very stoic small talk in between. I was convinced my mother loved me more.

As for tears on visiting days? Well, I couldn't tell you exactly when they stopped, I can only say they stopped a lot earlier on the outside than they did on the inside.

Evenings of visiting Sundays were always particularly exciting. Everybody wanted to know what presents everyone else got, and we compared and shared all kinds of games, toys and goodies. Almost all the girls had visitors, but on some occasions, there might be one or two girls who received no visitors at all. It happened to me only once, and I was devastated. The following month my mother told me she was beside herself when she realized too late in the day it was my visiting Sunday. Josie, by then, came infrequently and was not likely to remind her. I forgave her in an instant and was so grateful it never happened again. She kept "that" promise.

Naturally the girls were always heartsick when they didn't have visitors, and Sister would spend the entire visiting time with them so they didn't feel alone. Afterwards, she even seemed particularly kinder to them, in spite of the fact that she herself was always very frazzled and overwhelmed when we got back after visiting hours. There were so many packages of new toys to deal with for so many children, a fact that would have a particular impact on me some time further down the road. Because it was so very hard for Sister to get us settled down for supper on visiting Sundays, the silence bell in the dining room got a major workout.

Before too long the men were putting the finishing touches on the pool, and I had a new navy blue bathing suit with a white gardenia on the upper left side just waiting for the big day. Each morning during Sister's rounds, we asked her if the weather was warm enough yet for the pool.

Her answer was always the same, "Pretty soon children, pretty soon."

Finally, after breakfast one hot July day, she announced, "Today you can all go into the pool".

We were almost wild with joy as we scrambled into our new suits and lined up to go outside. The sun felt scorching as we approached the new pool beckoning us with its spotless cold water. Stepping into it was very special for this little girl from the big city. We splashed and jumped up and down just like "normal" children would. Each of us, without needing to say it, knew that was exactly what the others were thinking.

Sister sat on the edge of the pool watching us as the wimple covering her forehead gradually darkened with perspiration along the edges. Nothing about her wardrobe seemed to change with the seasons, she wore the same amount of clothing all year long. Beneath the regular sleeves of her habit were undersleeves tight against her arms, which must have been unbearable in that heat, not to mention the long dress and stockings. I asked her why she couldn't take off her shoes and stockings and at least wet her feet in the pool. She was shocked by my suggestion, rolling her eyes back and looking utterly scandalized. It was the first time I felt genuinely sorry for her, and grateful she would bear such discomfort for our pleasure. I even felt a twinge of affection for her, but only a twinge. There weren't many times that summer when we were allowed in the pool, but on those few days we were, it was positively the most carefree fun Alicia and I could imagine.

As the days cooled, the leaves on the trees became more and more beautiful with each passing week. Soon we were engulfed in a panorama of burgundy, orange, scarlet and buttery yellow trees, each displaying the fullness of a bridal bouquet. Those same trees, which many months earlier had appeared like bars confining me inside a prison, were transforming into an exquisite landscape I could retreat to anytime I wanted. Noticing the beauty around me was my way of coping with the emptiness inside and longing for my home and family. This coping mechanism continued to work better and better as time went on.

Fall provided its own kind of fun things to do which, for children confined as we were, meant far more than it would for children in a normal environment. One day before we went on our afternoon walk, Sister provided us with large burlap bags, assigning several girls to each bag. We were going to have a contest, she said. Off we went for our walk along those very familiar paths lined with apple trees, the only difference being there were no longer any apples on the trees. Instead, they were strewn on the ground everywhere. I finally realized where all the applesauce came from. We had our own apple supply, and it was quite plentiful, certainly enough for many, many, more meals. Sister said to pick up the apples as fast as we could, and the team who filled their bag first would get a prize when we returned. Naturally, we weren't allowed to run around like we needed to, that was considered far too strenuous, but we did get our bags filled fairly quick. Alicia and I were on the same team, and we managed to hold our own with the older girls, but I don't recall our team winning, only that it was more fun than we had had since the pool days.

Afterwards, when we left our filled bags for the caretakers to pick up, we were actually happy to be going back to our building again. We even looked forward to what fun thing we might be able to do the next day, like visiting the rows of pumpkin patches. Those tiny little balls that had only peeked out at us from under broad, green leaves during the hot summer days had grown huge and deep orange, reminding us that Halloween was just around the corner.

One thing I'd become keenly aware of with the passing of time was the extraordinary bond between my sisters and myself. It grew more every day. One girl's pain was all of our pain, and one girl's joy was joyous to all of us. We were sharing an existence totally unique from children in the outside world.

When Sister tapped on the playroom door, blew her whistle outside, or rang the quiet bell in the dining room, she was invading our world. A world where we could share memories of home, gossip, or express our true feelings. On some level, we might have been compared to soldiers and how they experience their comrades. We were together every waking minute of every day, facing exactly the same struggles being in a place like ours presented. In a sense, we were more than sisters, we were one body. But, like all bodies, there was always a part, or parts, one is not too happy with.

For the girls in our building, the name of that part was Patty O'Malley, who always smelled of pee and had cold sticky fingers that seemed to never leave her blood-red lips. She also seemed to have an unusual curiosity regarding the human anatomy, which prompted her to peek at us through the cracks along the sides of the bathroom doors when we were in a toilet stall. This, of course, created real problems for the rest of us in light of Sister's endless lectures on the virtues of modesty. And it earned her the well-deserved title, "Piggy Patty." But, aside from Piggy Patty, all the girls got along amazingly well as we shared our unique cloistered experience together.

I was learning much about how to negotiate my environment, like the differences I observed in the behavior of children from different backgrounds. Early on it became clear that Irish girls were more confident and extremely proud of just being Irish, as if that alone made them superior. I found that to be a bit puzzling, and more than a little enviable. The Italian girls tended to be shy, passive actually, but more affectionate once you got to know them. They were certainly not at all interested in being leaders. The Jewish girls seemed to feel they somehow needed to prove themselves all the time and were almost personally responsible for Christ's crucifixion. Observing these differences was fascinating to me. Without really having an understanding of what was happening, I was developing a rather rich inner life. There was so much time to think, observe and discern the actions and reactions of my environment on everyone around me, then come to some very plausible conclusions.

Sister Martha could never penetrate the bond between us, And I believe she knew that. There were times when I actually felt sorry for her. Hers was a hard and lonely life consisting almost entirely of taking care of us. From dawn till dusk she attended to our needs in one form or another with virtually no time for herself or the companionship of other adults. How could there be time, with full responsibility for twenty-five children under the age of ten? The more expected of her, the more she expected from us. How could it be otherwise? It was an unnatural life for all of us, yet it was far from a life without *meaning*.

Halloween was marked with lots of candy and decorations everywhere, but nothing to compare to the fun and excitement of trick-or-treating back home. When I reminded Sister of that on Halloween night as she rolled up my hair, up went those disapproving eyebrows. Sister disapproved of a lot of things, like sitting with one's legs crossed instead of knees together. She would call it "very un-lady like," a term she used a lot. Or if a woman wore red polish on her nails, those should be seen as the claws of the devil. Her list went on and on, but the message was always the same. Anything that didn't include suffering or sacrificing in one form or another was seen as wrong and there was something innately noble about pain and suffering. Even joy was suspect. As for love? Well, that was always akin to sacrifice. We absorbed these messages every day like dry, little sponges, and they would have far-reaching ramifications in our future lives and relationships.

Once Halloween was over, I started to think ahead to Thanksgiving, as I marked off the holidays to measure how long I was away from home. It was impossible to think I might still be there for Christmas. I'll be home for Christmas, I told myself. But when we were sitting in the beautifully decorated dining room, looking at papier-mâché pumpkins and Pilgrims everywhere and waiting for Sister to emerge from the kitchen with our turkey dinner, I started to have some panicky thoughts.

Was it possible God was not hearing my prayers? I could understand if that were true because, with so many people in the world to listen to, a little kid could easily go unnoticed. But would He actually betray me too? Maybe I'm not praying hard enough. That must be it! I'll just have to increase the number of Hail Marys and Our Fathers I pray at night. I decided the whole Rosary might do it. I realized we already said it almost every day, but concluded those prayers didn't count because we were already praying for the starving children in Europe, our soldiers fighting all over the world, and anyone else Sister could come up with. I had to get God's attention on me alone so He could concentrate on a miracle just for me. That's how I'll get home! So, out came the Rosary beads and prayer book Sister had given me on my First Holy Communion day, and under my pillow they both went, where they would remain for a very, very, long time.

Before I realized it, Christmas fever was upon us, and all we could think about was what to ask Santa to bring and whether or not he would know where to find us. Sister reassured us daily that he knew everything, and not to worry.

Yet, on visiting day, I thought it wise to beg Josie to write him a letter and tell him I wanted that rubber wetting doll we had both seen in a toy store window before I had gone away. I thought that doll was the most beautiful thing I had ever seen, and the fact she actually wet after a bottle made her that much more extraordinary. My sister promised she would get on it as soon as they got home and would absolutely include my change of address. I was convinced if I could at least have that doll, living at the hospital would be more tolerable.

The cold weather in the weeks before Christmas meant we never went outdoors. One morning, I was awakened by screeches of excitement from the girls on the opposite side of the aisle, whose beds were in front of the windows.

"Snow! Snow! It snowed last night, look!"

We all leaped out of our beds and ran to the windows. The scene was absolutely breathtaking. Everything was evenly covered, every branch and twig wrapped in a puffy white blanket stretching out as far as we could see, not a single human print to mar the exquisite perfection of nature's handiwork. All of us wished we could jump into the snow to our hearts content, the way we would have done if we were home. We fell silent as we stared out the windows, lost in our own memories. Then, for the first time in my life, I felt the unmistakable stillness a heavy snowfall can leave behind, penetrating through the glass pane my nose pressed against. When Sister came in pushing her temperature cart, we begged her to just let us go out long enough to make one snowball.

"Now girls, you all know you can't do that."

As I said, changes of any kind where not common in our daily lives. Yet once in a while Sister would come up with something she wanted to rearrange, like the morning she announced we would be changing dorms. I was being transferred to the dorm adjacent to the classroom with some other girls. It was almost like a regular moving day as we packed our belongings and shuffled back and forth to our new quarters. When I went to place my things in my new cabinet, I noticed immediately that one hinge on the heavy metal door was missing, leaving the door perilously hanging on only one hinge and making it very difficult to take things in and out. I told Sister as soon as I realized it. She said she knew about it and I would just have to do my best until she could get one of the caretakers to fix it.

Days went by, then weeks, without the door getting repaired. I tried to get used to the annoyance of it because every time I reminded Sister, she became more irritated. Eventually, with Christmas rushing towards us and rehearsals for the Christmas show, I had little time to worry about it. I had been picked to be featured in the show as the smallest angel to crawl out of a brick cardboard chimney and perform a choreographed dance with the older girls. I found it incredibly exciting to be on stage, and a totally new experience. Nothing was further from my mind as the days before Christmas dwindled down than that hanging cabinet door.

One evening after lights out, Sister came to the door and asked us to all get up quietly, line up, and follow her to the playroom for a special surprise. We clung to each other as we walked down the dark hall in absolute wonderment, speculating on what the surprise could possibly be. When we entered, Sister instructed us to go to the windows, where we saw the older girls from St. Mary's building were gathering. A light snow had started to fall. The tiny flakes looked like diamonds cascading down on the already snow-covered ground and gently resting on the heads and shoulders of the girls and nun. Some girls held fur muffs to keep their hands warm. Their house mother, Mother Mary Grace, clutched a thick white shawl around her shoulders with one hand, while holding a brightly lit gas lantern with the other. Then they all started to sing Christmas carols.

No Christmas card could ever depict the exquisite beauty I looked upon that evening, nor the lovely sounds of their voices echoing into the night. Tears welled up in my eyes as I thought of my mother and sister back home in the city, how they would never see such real beauty where they lived, and I actually felt sorry for them.

Sister leaned over my shoulder and asked, "Why are you crying Mary?"

For a moment I panicked, thinking she might punish me again for crying, but then I told her the truth, "I wish my mother and sister could see this Sister, it's so beautiful."

She said nothing, but pressed my shoulders tightly.

Finally, it was Christmas morning, and after weeks of built-up electrifying excitement, we were almost calm as we awaited the sound of Sister's cart rolling down the hall.

When she entered, she greeted us. "Merry Christmas, children."

"Merry Christmas, Sister Martha! Did Santa come last night?"

"Well of course he came!" Calmly, she shook the first thermometer from its vial.

"And was that Santa making all that noise in the playroom last night Sister? Was it?"

"Oh, I'm sure it was, along with his helpers. Now, I want you all to get dressed as quickly as you can so we can go to Mass. Then, after breakfast, we can all go into the playroom and see what Santa has brought each of you."

The chapel looked beautiful with a Christmas tree on one side of the altar and poinsettia flowers everywhere. We sang Christmas carols with the rest of the children during Mass, but all we could think about was the playroom and what it held for each of us. When we got back to St. Michael's after Mass, we waited outside the dining room for Sister. When she opened the door, we were shocked at how the room had been transformed. Beautiful wreaths hung at every window; each table was covered with a bright red and green tablecloth and had a lovely miniature Christmas tree in the center. Disappointingly, nothing changed on the menu except for fresh fruit salad instead of juice.

When breakfast was over, Mother Superior appeared with her assistant, Mother Katherine, to help Sister with the Christmas gifts. We were each given a small piece of paper with two numbers written on it. When the door of the playroom was opened, we were in absolute awe. It looked like a Christmas wonderland with decorations everywhere. The Christmas tree was huge, with a star pressed tight against the ceiling, branches that extended out further than I had ever seen before in my life, and the most unique ornaments imaginable.

Under the tree sat rows of beautiful dolls, all in hand-knitted outfits completely different from each other, along with piles of beautifully wrapped boxes of every size. The nuns looked on with great satisfaction, saying nothing as they reveled in our joyful reactions. One nun picked up the first doll, called out the number written on it, and its owner shouted with joy to claim her. And so it went, until all the dolls and boxes had been given away. There were wrappings and ribbons flying everywhere and squeals of joyful laughter, louder than I would have ever imagined I would hear in that room. But, it was Christmas morning in Saint Michael's building; the nuns had worked very hard to make it as beautiful as they could for us, and we were happy.

I was probably far too young to be anxious about being on stage for a Christmas show. All my attention was focused on whether or not my mother and Josie would have the special doll Santa brought me. I had even picked out a name for her: Susie. However, after Christmas dinner was over, excitement started to build at the prospect of putting on the show for our parents and nuns. No one dared fall asleep during naptime, and before we knew it we were on our way to the auditorium.

Sister brought me backstage to put on my angel outfit over my clothes, then the music started. I poked my head out of the chimney and saw the audience for the first time. They looked like a sea of faces, with Santa sitting in the first row, a nun on each side of him, one of whom was Mother Superior. I remained frozen on my hands and knees, hearing only the loud sound of oohs and ahhs from the audience, while Sister waved frantically from the sidelines for me to come out further from the fireplace. An older angel behind me provided the necessary shove, and out I popped.

We twirled around with brightly colored streamers flowing from our hands, and it seemed to me the audience was doing an awful lot of giggling for what I considered to be a very serious performance. When it was over, the applause was deafening. Sister pulled me aside, removed my angel outfit and brought me back on stage where Santa (who, I would later discover, was Dr. Tara) had come to the foot of the stage and extended his hand to me. I lowered my hand once, withdrew, tried again, but finally turned around, and just buried my face in Sister's dress. It seemed no matter what I did the audience found it incredibly amusing. Very strange behavior for grownups. What is wrong with these people? I thought at the time.

The outfit Sister dressed me in that day was a bright yellow dress with matching underpants edged with white lace ruffles. She lifted me up in her arms and carried me down the aisle where my mother and sister waited. When I saw my mother's face, it was beet red and swollen with large blotches, even down to her neck. Josie's face was almost as red and swollen.

"Mommy! Josie! What's the matter with your faces?" I gasped.

"Oh, you looked so beautiful up there, it just made us cry a little," Josie said.

They both clutched wrinkled, wet handkerchiefs in their hands. A little? I had never seen their faces look like that in my entire life. I found the scene very puzzling, but not enough to question them any further — I had Susie on my mind.

A bulging shopping bag sat at my mother's feet, and she couldn't wait to give me the largest box. As I tore off the wrapping, I recognized at once the small suitcase that had held Susie in the store window. Sure enough, when

I unlatched it, there she was. My heart almost exploded out of my chest with joy.

"He found my house!" was all I could shout.

My mother and sister were beaming. Slowly, I untied the doll from its pinnings and held her in my arms, unleashing an unexpected burst of emotion. I became overwhelmed with a feeling of protectiveness for that little pink rubber doll I held.

My mind dashed back to our playroom where there were already a number of body parts from headless and limbless dolls stacked on the book-case shelves. Dolls who lost their battle in unre-solved quarrels for possession. That will never happen to my Susie, I told myself. I could still exercise at least that much power. By sending the doll home I would be creating a real con-nection with everything I left behind. My doll could become an extension of myself, the part that would be where I longed to be, allowing me to feel less separated. As psychologists would agree, I'm sure, it was a classic case of transfer-ence.

I turned to my mother, "You have to take her home again Mommy, where she will be safe.

The other children will only break her here. I just know they will."

My mother looked at me with a mixture of both pain and horror, while at the same time spotting Sister Martha walking down the aisle.

She waved frantically and called out, "Sister, Sister!"

"No! No! Mommy please, please don't tell her what I said!" But she was determined, and before I could utter another word, Sister was standing over us asking my mother what the problem was.

"Sister, my daughter tells me the children here break toys, and she wants me to bring this beautiful doll she wanted so much back home with me today. Is it true? Do the children really break everything Sister?"

As if Sister would have said, "Oh yes, of course they do."

Sister's lips remained smiling, a smile that never reached her eyes, where the corners were crinkled tight as she looked down at me with an icy stare that promised a revengeful rebuke would be forthcoming. A beautiful Christmas was rapidly turning ugly.

"No, Mrs. D'Agostino the children don't break toys here. Don't you want to share, Mary?"

I nodded yes, but I knew I couldn't share Susie, I already loved her too much. She had to go home, where she would be safe, no matter how hard it was to let her go. I could wait until I got well to be with her again. My baby was going home even if I couldn't. My mother was totally crushed, but I refused to change my mind. Besides, I already had been given a very nice doll to play with and share with my sisters, and that was the end of it. Or so I thought.

I watched Sister very closely for the next few days, wondering about the repercussions of my decision. I almost thought there might not be any. Then one evening while I struggled to get my things in my cabinet and balance the broken door at the same time, the hinge finally gave way. The door fell off completely, crashing loudly to the floor. The girls in my room started shouting for Sister, and I could hear her keys jingling and the sound of her cotton sneakers running down the hall.

"What was that noise?" she asked breathlessly.

"Mary's cabinet door fell off, Sister," a chorus of girls volunteered.

Sister moved to the center of the aisle while she motioned with her right index finger for me to come forward. I couldn't imagine what for. When I stood beside her, she roughly turned me around to face all the girls in my dorm.

"Children, I want your attention. On Christmas Day, Mary forced her mother to take home the doll Santa brought her because she didn't want to share it with the rest of you. She was afraid you would break her doll, but, it's fine when she breaks our hospital property."

Why is she lying? She knew the door was always broken!

"Now, what should we say about that, children?" she screeched.

"But...but...you knew all the time!" I pleaded.

"Silence! You should be ashamed of yourself, young lady, now get right back into your bed."

All of the girls in the dorm stared at me with sheer contempt, except for the ones on either side of my bed who knew the door had been broken when it was assigned to me. So, nuns can lie right to your face. I wondered if she would confess that to Father Fitzgerald on Saturday. I imagined her saying, "Bless me Father for I have sinned. I lie all the time to sick, innocent children."

But Sister Martha had other sins to confess.

೦಼ಿ೦

The year was winding down fast. Soon it would be gone, and I was still at All Saints wondering if I would ever go home again. My daydreams started to change, I saw myself all grown up, becoming a nun and living there permanently. Or, even better, maybe becoming one of those ladies in white coats who looked into their microscopes in the laboratory and put different colored liquids in thin, tall vials. There was something incredibly intoxicating about that prospect.

It was especially intoxicating on dark, cold, rainy days, when I would stare out the classroom window, pretending to be sharpening my pencil in the sharpener on the window sill as the rain pelted down hard against the pane and drenched the earth below. I could see those dimly lit windows of the laboratory across the grounds and I knew the ladies in white were down there all cozy and insulated from the world like I was. The difference was they were doing something very important and, in the evening, they were free to go home to be with their families in that whole other world.

A world where there were movies, hotdogs, Kosher pickles that came out of large wooden barrels with garlic cloves floating in circles around them, French fries with ketchup, streetcars coming and going, bakery windows filled with all kinds of cakes to choose from. Those ladies were free, and yet protected while surrounded by the beauty and serenity of the sanatorium. That became my dream.

"Mary dear, please come away from the window now and take your seat like a good little girl."

Why did Mrs. Hurst always have to interrupt my favorite daydream?

Winter dragged on, with blustery winds and high snow drifts the girls and I could only look at with longing. Sometimes we would catch a glimpse of a nun wrapped in a thick wool shawl from her neck to her knees, half bent over, braving the winds and swirling snow circling around her as she struggled towards her destination. What a beautiful ethereal vision in white that image burned in my memory.

The only thing to really look forward to was my birthday at the end of February. I was going to be seven, which was supposed to be some kind of milestone, at least that's what I was told. "The age of reasoning," I think Sister called it. But all I wondered about was what kind of gifts would I get from home, and what would it be like to have a birthday at the hospital.

Throughout the year there had been other birthdays, and the children didn't seem too disturbed about not being at home for their special day. But then the children never seemed to be upset about anything, always leaving me with a feeling there must be something wrong with me. I marveled at how adjusted, or, should I say resigned, they were to living at the hospital, and I truly tried very hard to be more like them.

Sometimes it actually worked, other times it didn't. The truth is, children can almost always appear to look happy even when internally they are undergoing the most traumatic experience, something no one understands at age six — and some adults never understand.

In the meantime, I continued to focus on learning to better enjoy whatever was in my immediate world. Like those Thursday evenings when we were allowed to create our own entertainment. After our cold suppers, while munching on our candy, we could tell stories or volunteer to sing in the front of the dining room under the dinner bell. This is where I discovered I had a voice. One evening, while Sister was washing off the tables, I hit a difficult note in a song. Maybe it was "Somewhere Over the Rainbow," the children liked that one. I saw those eyebrows of hers go up. *She thinks I'm good.* She didn't even have to say it, I was learning to read her body language. The times when she could shock me with her erratic behavior, like my first night in the dorm with the pillow incident, were becoming fewer and further apart. Actually, most of the time, I could read her straight on. And that, to me, spelled power.

It was visiting Sunday, and the following day was my seventh birthday. My mother arrived with a big white box and I knew it held my cake. She was very excited about this particular cake and said I would be so surprised when I saw how its top had been decorated, because it was very different from any cake I had ever had in my life. My curiosity was definitely piqued. What could this cake possibly look like? As visiting time moved along, all she could do was remind me over and over again how careful I needed to be carrying my cake back to our building. I promised her profusely that I would be very careful and not to worry. We parted in the same frenzy of hugs and kisses as we always did, but more that day, since it would be my first birthday away from home.

The walk back to St. Michael's held the same excitement every visiting day did, with everyone holding on to their new treasures and talking at the same time. We lined up outside the dining room where Sister told us to pile our boxes one on top of the other, so we could reclaim them after supper. I held on to my cake box assuming there was no way she meant my box, since I had already told her it held my birthday cake and she knew the weight of the other boxes would crush it. While most of the girls placed their boxes on the floor and went into the dining room as ordered, some girls were not moving quite quickly enough for Sister, so she poked hard at their shoulders or pulled at their hair to speed things along.

Sister was becoming more and more agitated, tossing back her veil wildly and almost screaming at us to place our packages down, "NOW!"

I held on to mine as long as I could, trying desperately to remind her again that mine needed to go into the kitchen, but to no avail. She pointed to the pile, mouthing the word "NOW." I knew this look well, so I placed my box on the floor next to the original piles just hoping no one would put theirs on top of it. I watched, as one, two, three, more boxes piled on my birthday cake box. The lid dented down slowly, until it gradually began to cave. I silently turned away, and went to my assigned seat at my table.

The next day Mrs. Hurst had placed a card on my desk and I felt very special because she had remembered. I thought about little else during that morning in class except whether my cake had survived the weight placed on it the evening before, and what was so special about the cake my mother wouldn't tell me. Afternoon mealtime proceeded without Sister ever mentioning my birthday, let alone the birthday cake, but I didn't worry about it since I was certain she would bring it out for dessert after supper.

We went in for our naps as usual, then into the playroom afterwards where Sister handed out our mail. There were cards from my Mother and Josie, and I was very happy to share them with Alicia and the other girls who knew it was my birthday.

They all asked the same question. "Didn't your mother bring your birthday cake yesterday?"

I told them it was probably going to be served after supper. Before I could say another word, Sister was tapping her ring on the glass in the door, summoning us to line up for supper.

When supper was finished, my anticipation took over, prompting me to ask, "Sister aren't we going to have my birthday cake for dessert?"

It was the first time she had looked at me all day. "That cake was too crushed to put candles on, so I decided to share what was left of it with the other nuns rather than throw it away," she mumbled.

I dropped my face to hide the tears welling up, but she could still see how disappointed I was. So, once again, she attempted to shame me in front of the other girls. "Do you mind that I let the nuns enjoy what was left of your cake, Mary?"

Mind? Of course I mind, you stupid woman! That was MY birthday cake, not theirs. It was for my seventh birthday — the one YOU told me was sooo special — the age of reasoning! You are a cruel and evil woman, Sister Martha! I HATE you!

"No Sister, it's okay."

I watched her disappear into her kitchen and emerge with a tray of dishes holding those wretched prunes. Before serving them, however, she turned to the other children and said, "Children, today is Mary D'Agostino's birthday, I want you all to sing 'Happy Birthday' to her."

❦

On visiting day, the first thing my mother asked was, "How was your birthday? What did you think of that beautiful cake?"

I told her the story, and she was incredulous. She kept repeating, "No, no, that can't be! It was such a beautiful cake, and I paid so much for it too. Those animals, the nerve…"

She was mumbling then to herself, "Well, she must have…at least let you…"

"No Mommy, I never tasted the cake. I never even saw it! Do you understand?"

My mother looked around slowly, as if she were hoping someone from somewhere would appear and rescue her from my words. Since that didn't happen, she accepted her defeat, and asked hopefully, "Did she at least do something else for you, bella mamma?"

"Yes, Sister let the children sing Happy Birthday, then we ate prunes for dessert."

The Incident

In a dark time, the eye begins to see.

THEODORE ROETHKE

Patient turnover at the sanatorium was very slow, months could go by without a single child leaving. But before one did, there was always the same ritual. First you were called aside and presented with a jar to urinate in. Then, after a day or so, you were brought to the hospital building where that silent, homely, lady doctor would examine you alone and take several vials of blood. Another day or two might go by and, without warning, Sister would announce that so-and-so would be going home today. That was the way it was done. The adjusting was left to us and it was usually very hard. Sometimes, it almost felt like a limb had been ripped off, depending on how close you had become. After a child left, the building was always very quiet, like we had lost a member of the family.

One day, one of our girls was replaced by a new girl. I'll call her Amy. A frail child with large dark eyes and dark hair, her skin was colorless, and if she was frightened, she hid it well in her expressionless face. She came to us from the hospital building, as did most of the other children. She watched us closely to learn all the different directions we followed, just as I had once done myself. In the evening, when we were all happily sharing our toys and secrets, I noticed Amy would just lie back on her pillows and stare at us vacantly, never saying a word. She struck me as being very, very, tired.

There was something else different about Amy. She couldn't hold down her food, and she threw up more than any of us ever did. When we announced, "Sister Martha, Amy just threw up!" Sister would automatically come out of the kitchen, armed with her dishrag, and wipe it up. This went on for perhaps a week or more, before Sister had become convinced Amy was making herself throw up.

"You're forcing yourself to throw up," she shouted at her, while Amy tearfully protested, "No Sister I'm not. I really can't help it, I just can't."

Where would an adult get such a strange idea, that a child would force herself to vomit? I wondered if maybe she had had an earlier experience with someone who actually did that. It was the only explanation that made any sense. I remembered the times at home when the rheumatic fever was at its worst and I threw up all the time. It was the worst part of the illness. Why would a child do it deliberately? At night, I thought about these things before I fell asleep. In my very young mind, I was coming to the conclusion that perhaps something might be wrong with Sister. She forbade us to cough, insisting we could control that too, so if we had to cough at night, we did so under our pillows.

Would my mother have believed me if I told her these things? Of course not, she was totally trusting of my environment and everyone in it. Why wouldn't she be? Every visiting day I observed how increasingly more relaxed she appeared. Her face no longer displayed the tension and stress once so familiar to me. My mother was very comfortable with my placement. It was a place which provided an abundance of good food, fresh air and plenty of bed rest. At the time, those were the only remedies available for children with sick hearts. Penicillin, the drug that would wipe out rheumatic fever and other diseases forever, was not yet available. Whatever the hospital provided, it did so very well. Still, it could never be guaranteed everyone caring for us could meet the emotional needs we all had, or that they would even try. This was something my mother never considered — emotional damage was not a popular topic in the 1940s.

As for the children? I suspect we were demonstrating Stockholm Syndrome, where a person actually comes to love her controller rather than have nothing at all to cling to. All of us were very much under Sister Martha's influence and not about to rebel or question anything she said or did.

I hoped Amy could stop vomiting, for her sake and for ours. But she didn't stop, and one day after wiping up her mess, Sister's frustration and accusations turned to threats.

"The next time you throw up, young lady, you're going to be very, very, sorry," she hissed through her gritted teeth.

The girls at my table and the other tables snickered behind their hands at the absurdity of her remark because she could be very dramatic at times, especially when she wanted to make a point. However, that day I did not find her very amusing as I gazed at Amy, whose face reflected the utter helplessness she was feeling.

The day proceeded without further episodes, and I felt genuine relief for Amy, who actually tried to join us in the playroom later, appearing somewhat brighter. The next morning started as usual, and Amy seemed herself. I felt like life at St. Michael's remained undisturbed as we filed into the dining room for breakfast. The chatter at the breakfast tables was lively that morning, and Sister needed to ring the bell several times because the noise had exceeded the acceptable level.

Suddenly, I heard someone at Amy's table shout those familiar words, "Sister Martha, Amy just threw up again!"

Dead silence fell instantly over all of us as we watched the kitchen door swing open and

Sister emerge with dishrag in hand. I didn't like what I was reading in her body language. She walked steady and expressionless over to Amy's table and slowly and deliberately moved aside the other children's bowls so she could gather up the vomit into one neat pile. Silently, she placed Amy's bowl under the edge of the table and mopped the vomit back into it with her dishrag. No one breathed as she took Amy's spoon, plunged it into the vomit with a sickening plopping sound, and slid the bowl in front of her.

"Now, eat it!"

The rest of us, in unison, released a loud gasp as we looked on in complete horror. I can't recall if Amy made any kind of vocal protest, but her eyes stared wildly down at the bowl. Even her tears had stopped falling.

Sister turned to leave, but not before informing Amy, "You will sit there until you do."

The rest of our breakfast time went by without a sound, other than our spoons hitting the sides of the bowls followed by the shuffling of chairs as we slid them neatly under our tables before lining up for the trip down the hall to the classroom. We had to pass behind Amy's chair as we filed out of the room, and that could only be described as surreal.

Later, as we sat at our desks, Mrs. Hurst — who had no idea what we had just witnessed, nor would she ever have believed it — observed how exceptionally quiet we were that morning. Each girl was lost in her own thoughts with the same question: "Will she really make Amy eat her own vomit?"

My thoughts at the time ran along the lines of wanting to tell someone. Doing what she did to an already sick child was something so despicable it needed to be exposed, yet how could I ever be the one courageous enough to do it? I decided it had to be buried along with everything else I had witnessed.

Class was over, and we were lining up for dinner. Each of us hoped Amy wouldn't still be sitting over her vomit bowl, but when we got there, she was just as we had left her hours earlier. She looked up at us beseechingly, and I felt my stomach turn over several times before it dropped. The tables were set and Sister was rushing about as usual, as if nothing was any different from any other meal. She placed our plates in front of us and we said grace, each of us trying very hard not to look at Amy. I wondered how the other children at her table were expected to eat while she stared at her breakfast bowl of vomit.

It may have been at dinner, or it could very well have also been at supper, when we finally saw the look of sheer relief on Amy's face as Sister came over to her and removed the bowl without saying a word. Minutes later Amy's expression changed again, this time to determination, when Sister returned with a plate of fresh food.

I prayed silently for her to hold down the new food and believed it would happen, until I heard that dreaded shriek once more, "Sister Martha, Amy just threw up again!"

Sister came out of the kitchen, dishrag and container in hand, and silently wiped up the new mess. Amy stared vacantly off in space, her face completely blank. After that day, we never saw Amy again.

We had to ask Sister where Amy was because she never volunteered information, and she told us Amy had been transferred back to the hospital building. A couple days later, she asked us to include Amy in our prayers so she would get well soon. It was this kind of behavior that made it very difficult to believe in my own reality. At night, I would think about her actions and wonder how could it be possible for an adult to not know there was something wrong with Amy, when I was only seven years old at the time and I knew it. Weren't we all there because something was wrong with us? Why was the child punished for what might have been a symptom of her illness? I would try desperately to make sense out of the actions of a woman who seemed to be different from the other nuns. But at seven you don't understand that, nor do you have the luxury to even hate the person for her actions, because you're probably experiencing some kind of syndrome. I prayed hard for Amy the night of the incident, while promising myself I would never forgive Sister Martha for what she had done.

The following weekend was visiting Sunday, and the events of the week were very much on the minds of each child. None of us really discussed Amy very much, as if nothing ever happened — typical behavior for those who are powerless. But we all knew it had happened.

After eating our usual Sunday roast chicken dinner and napping afterwards, we were lining up in the hall for our trip to the auditorium to see our parents. I watched Sister closely all that day because she seemed rather edgy, particularly as we were getting ready to leave. She kept pacing back and forth, not giving us permission to proceed down the stairs. Finally, she stopped pacing, and I knew exactly what was coming.

"Girls, I want your attention before we go down to the auditorium. Remember, everything that goes on here at St. Michael's is our business, because this is our house, and we don't tell anybody outside what goes on in our house. Do you understand that perfectly?"

"Yes Sister," we responded in unison.

I was right, she knew she had done something very wrong, and she wanted to ensure no one else would know. And, they didn't.

Easter was coming, my second one at the hospital. Thoughts about Amy no longer haunted me like they once had, and it seemed I had almost forgotten her. At least that's what I thought. In religion class, Sister's instructions were filled with stories of the crucifixion. Sister talked about Lent and how we needed to make as many sacrifices as we could during this special time, and offer them up to Jesus. She talked about filling up our own Easter basket for Him in our hearts with all the really special sacrifices we made, so we could present them to Jesus on Easter Sunday morning. Some of the girls decided they would give up candy or gum, or anything else they particularly liked.

This caused a dilemma for me, since there was virtually nothing in the way of food or candy I cared enough about to feel it would be a sacrifice to give up. True, I had discovered some foods I actually liked. There was baked macaroni and cheese for instance, which I found quite delicious. Coming from an Italian family, I had never seen any kind of macaroni that wasn't red, so macaroni and cheese was a real surprise. As for puddings, chocolate was the only one I loved, the rest were all disgusting to me, especially tapioca pudding with all those translucent dots in it. Besides, Sister would come unglued if

I refused anything that even looked like food. She would think it was only an excuse not to eat, not fasting. I talked to Alicia about my dilemma, hoping she might come up with something, but she was of no help at all, and the days were dwindling fast.

Easter was about a week away when I thought I had found the perfect gift for my Jesus basket. We had just finished dinner and were waiting for Sister to appear with our desserts. When she came out, she was holding a tray full of dessert dishes filled with tapioca pudding. My stomach turned over once before it occurred to me this might just be the chance I was looking for to put something truly special in my Jesus basket. When she placed the dish in front of me, I already had my spoon in hand, ready to dig in. Washing every spoonful down with a swig of milk, I ate the entire dish and even scraped the sides clean.

"Seconds anyone?" Sister called out.

Several girls happily raised their hands. I had never, ever, asked for seconds of anything the whole time I was there, nor would I probably ever have. But, I thought, if I can do this, my basket will have the best gift of all for Jesus, and

He will surely answer my prayers to go home. Ever so slowly, I raised my hand and watched Sister's face light up like a Christmas bulb.

When she came out of her kitchen, she headed straight for me with a towering dish of tapioca pudding that actually hung over the sides and undulated with every step she took before she placed it square down in front of me. I sucked in a very deep breath and picked up my spoon, staring at the mountain of glistening dots.

"I'm doing this for you, Sweet Jesus."

"Sister Martha, Mary just threw up all over everything!"

My ears heard the words, but my mind could not take them in, because my lunch was exploding out of every orifice of my face. In an instant she was standing there, one hand on the back of the chair of the girl next to me, the other on her hip, her eyes bulging with rage. Amy flashed across my mind, and I felt faint.

"Why did you ask for seconds?" she screamed.

"For my…my…basket."

"What? What basket? What are you talking about?"

"The Easter basket you told us to fill for Jesus. I ate all that pudding I hate so much for Him, and now I have nothing for Him. I have nothing at all, His basket is empty...it's empty!" I managed to sputter through gulping, suffocating tears.

It was the only sound that broke the silence in the room. When I finally looked up and saw her face, she was a woman transformed. Her eyes had softened, the muscles of her cheeks had slackened, one hand was down at her side, and the other just resting on the back of the girl's chair. Sister appeared to be internally struggling with herself, as she finally straightened her shoulders.

"Mary, go into the bathroom and clean yourself up." Those were the only words she could half-whisper to me.

"Yes Sister, sorry Sister."

I scrambled out of my chair, and ran from that room with the speed of a bullet. That night I prayed for Amy again, asking Jesus to please make her well enough to go home, or at least to another building. I also promised I would keep working on His Easter basket.

During that time, Amy was not the only one to leave us unexpectedly. One Saturday afternoon as we all sat cross-legged on the floor of the playroom waiting for Father Fitzgerald to listen to our confession, Sister walked in with a new priest. She told us Father Fitzgerald was sick and he wouldn't be able to come by and hear our confessions. We didn't think very much about it until the following week, when the same thing happened.

Then one rainy afternoon, when Sister was doing what we loved most, sitting on the piano stool telling us stories, she said she had something sad to tell us.

"Girls, Father Fitzgerald will not be coming back, he is in the hospital and is very ill. The doctors had to remove one of his legs. I want you all to pray very hard for him."

We were stunned and heartbroken. It was impossible to believe we would never see those twinkling blue eyes, or watch him perform his magic tricks after all the confessions had been heard on Saturday afternoons. Who would pull nickels from behind my left ear? He was the one who provided most of the fun for our week, and I loved him very much.

It was not long after her announcement that she told us Father had died, and she handed out his mass cards with his picture on it. Some of the children wept openly at the news, and I was one of them. I cannot tell you anything about the new priest, not even what he looked like. He must not have made any particular impression on me. Or perhaps my heart had only one special room for Father Fitzgerald, and that room was closed forever.

VII

The Visitors

The main reason for healing is love.

PARACELSUS (1493-1541)

It was around midsummer of my second or third year at the sanatorium when again, the men were busy building something in the play area. This time it was to be a playhouse, large enough for two to three children to play inside at the same time. When it was finished, we all raced over to the tree-shaded area where it stood and gazed at it in awe. The small structure had several shuttered windows, cedar shingles around its frame and a bright red door. It was truly impressive. The inside of the house was bare, except for a doll's crib with sides that went up and down just like a real baby's crib. Each of us couldn't wait to put our dolls in the crib and play house in a way that would provide us with an escape into our fantasy worlds never before imagined.

The following Sunday was visiting day and my mother, who had gained a reputation for bringing me the most unique toys, outdid herself when she came in with a very real-looking toy kitchen sink. It was about two feet high with a small water pan behind the faucet, providing running water that drained into another pan under the sink. I was sure my mother loved me more than anyone else's mother did to come up with something so unique. Sister was also impressed when she lingered long enough to see it, interrupting her casual stroll up and down the auditorium aisles. She commented on how nicely it would add to our collection of toys in the playroom. But I had another idea for my special sink, and when I told Sister I thought it should go into our playhouse, she agreed with me more emphatically than I had ever seen her do before. My mother, of course, was thrilled with her purchase and the nature of its timeliness. Later that week the sink went into the playhouse and the children were ecstatic to be able to actually splash water on our play dishes.

One day, just before it was my turn to play in the house with another girl for approximately ten minutes, I heard Sister calling, "Mary, Mary, come with me right now. I want to show you something."

"But Sister, I'll miss my turn," I pleaded.

"Don't worry, it will only take a few minutes, then you can be first in line again."

The two of us walked back towards our building, and my mind wondered, Could this be it? Is she going to ask me to pee in the bottle? Am I going home? Suddenly, she stopped just outside our building and asked me to look up at the sky at an airplane. When I did, there was no airplane, or bird, or anything else for that matter, just blue sky and blinding sun.

"I don't see anything, Sister, could we go back now please? I'm going to miss my turn."

"Look, look, I just saw it again," she said as she gently lifted my chin up.

Then she straightened my socks, retied my shoelaces, lifted my dress, tucked my undershirt tightly into my underpants, and turned me around so she could redo the bow on the back of my dress, all the while I'm wondering why I couldn't at least be in a building with a normal nun.

"What did you want to show me Sister? Is it upstairs in the dorm?"

"Oh, very well," she said, "maybe some other time I'll show you when you're not waiting for your turn in the new playhouse. We can walk back now."

That evening, after I rolled up the rag curls for some of the girls in my dorm (a job I had finally convinced Sister I could do as well as she did), Sister stood waiting for me in the doorway of the dorm so she could roll up my hair. Silence hovered around us like a shroud as she rolled each section of my hair around the wet rag. Finally, she spoke.

"Mary, when was the last time you saw your father?"

"Oh, I don't know."

"You don't know?"

"It was a long time ago, Sister, when I was just little."

"You mean you don't know where your own father is?"

"My mother told me he's in the army with my brother, that's all I know."

Sister finished rolling up my hair in silence and handed me back my comb and ribbon. I had started to walk back to my bed when she called after me.

"Mary?"

I half turned around. "Yes, Sister?"

"Your father, he loves you very, very, much. I want you to always remember that."

"Oh, I know that," I said, as I skipped down the aisle to my bed.

But, how did I know that? I thought to myself as I lay in bed staring at the dark ceiling after lights out. I started to go over the events of the day, like I did every night before drifting off to sleep. I recalled how Sister walked me right up to the windows and stopped directly in front of our dorm. Suddenly, her extra bizarre behavior made sense. Papa was here today. He was probably standing right at that window opposite my bed, watching me while Sister fussed with my clothes. She was showing me off to him, that's what she was doing. But he didn't want me to see him, and I knew precisely the reason why.

It had happened about a year or so before I entered All Saints Hospital, when I was not quite five. I remember my father and I on a subway train. He was taking me to a hospital in New York City, where I would remain for two months. It was the hospital my mother had always referred to in her promise. I was extremely angry at him, not only because he was bringing me to a hospital, but because I felt he had no rights at all where I was concerned. He didn't even live with us. How dare he be the one to take me away from my home. I was determined to hurt him as much as I was hurting. I decided the best way to do that was to show no emotion at all, not even to kiss him good-bye when the time came for us to separate. No one could force me to do that, it was the only shred of autonomy I had.

When we entered the hospital, we were greeted by a nurse who took down all the information concerning my health. I made no protest of any kind, while I could tell my father was coming apart internally. Then the nurse told him we needed to go upstairs. My father dutifully picked me up and followed closely behind her as he climbed the tall stairway.

At the top she said, "All right, Mr. D'Agostino, I'll take her now."

I let go of his hand, and took hers without ever looking back.

Suddenly, she stopped. "Oh my goodness, child, you forgot to kiss your father good-bye."

I turned around slowly. He was standing on the top stair, still holding on to the banister. I walked over to him, and coldly lifted my right cheek for him to kiss. He looked like someone who had just been stabbed through the heart might look. I felt so satisfied that I had, indeed, hurt him.

So, I understood completely why he chose for me not to see him that day. He was afraid I would reject him again, and that would have been too much for him to bear. It would be many years before I learned I had been right. But, on that night, I just rolled over on my side and fell instantly asleep, knowing for certain what Sister said was true: My father did love me.

ʚ̃ɞ

I realized he loved me even earlier than that, when I was about four. We lived in a three-story tenement building on the third floor. On most Saturday mornings, there was a gentle knock on the kitchen door. When my mother opened it, a young boy from the neighborhood would tell her, "There's a man downstairs who says he wants to see the baby."

If I was well enough to go out, my mother would tell one of my brothers to get ready to take me downstairs to see Papa, and to tell him to buy groceries. When Papa saw me, he'd lift me up in his arms and hold me close. No gushy kisses, just a long, silent hug, leaving me wondering, *So when is he going to put me down?* Then my brother Tony would give him the message that we needed to go food shopping.

"Yes, yes, we go to A&P store," he'd eagerly agree.

"Momma said you need to take the stroller too, because the baby can't walk too far."

"No, no, I carry her, no carriage." My father, being very Italian in his thinking, would never be seen dead pushing a child's stroller.

Although I hardly knew him, there were certain things about him that always came easily to mind. Papa wore a gray fedora hat, no matter what the temperature. The reason had more to do with him being strikingly bald, when baldness was definitely not stylish, than it did with the weather. Yet, in spite of his baldness, he was a rather good-looking man, with his warm brown eyes and fair, even skin tone. He always wore suspenders, so he could leave the top button of his trousers unbuttoned, and he wore long-sleeved white cotton shirts with their cuffs rolled up to his elbows.

My father loved to pace while he smoked his Camel cigarettes. He would walk back and forth for hours, one hand cupping his cigarette, the other hand behind him. Or, he would sit by the window for hours thinking before he'd turn around and speak to anyone who would listen to some keen insight he had about the human condition. My father's appearance was far from imposing, he was not tall, and a bit round-shouldered. He was a man who could easily be overlooked, which most of the time he was.

So, off to the A&P store the three of us went that day. Tony making sure Papa bought him the largest jar of peanut butter the store had, and I reminding him to buy me Yankee Doodles. It was something he was greatly delighted in doing. When we had bought as much as they could manage to carry along with carrying me, we headed home. Papa would preach incessantly to my brother all the way, and I could tell Tony wasn't listening to a word he was saying. When it was time to part, he did the same as he had done earlier, he would hold me very close for several long minutes before putting me down. Then in a shaky voice, he would remind me to force myself to eat as much as I could. I guess I wasn't listening either.

Papa would not be the only unscheduled visitor during that period, there would be others, and I was very pleased to see them.

For entertainment on the non-visiting Sundays, we always went to the auditorium to watch movies. Sometimes they were cartoons or Charlie Chaplin movies, but most of the time we watched a movie called The Song of Bernadette, my most favorite of all. It was on one of those Sundays that Mother Superior came walking down the aisle and over to Sister Martha. She whispered something in her ear which resulted in Sister telling me I had to leave with Mother Superior. Now. Of course, it was right in the middle of the best part of the movie, the part where Bernadette is just about to see the Virgin Mary on the grotto. But, at the same time, it was heartening to see Mother Superior actually beaming as the two of us left the auditorium.

"Where are we going Mother?"

"I can't tell you Mary, it's a surprise."

"A surprise? Am I going home?"

"Oh no, no, it's not that kind of surprise, but you'll be very happy anyway, you'll see."

Walking as quickly as I could to keep up with her, I noticed we were heading towards a room in the hospital building where we went about once a month during the winter to get tanned from the tanning lights in the ceiling. Another thing my mother could be completely thrilled about when she visited. It was a room that was totally empty, except for the mats on the floor for us to lie on after we had already undressed down to our underpants. What possible surprise could that room ever hold for me? I wondered. But, sure enough, she stopped right outside that door and asked, "Are you ready?"

I nodded a hesitant yes, and she slowly opened the door.

There the three of them sat, in an empty room waiting for me. My three siblings. I gasped when I saw them, my heart overwhelmed with love, and feeling more than a little pity for them too. They looked so scared and stiff in their chairs as Mother Superior backed away saying, "Here she is, your baby sister. Now have a nice visit with her and I'll be back later."

Tears burst out of me before she even closed the door. My sister, who had visited me so many times before, felt she knew why I was crying and acted very much like the mother figure.

"Now Mary, if you're going to keep crying to go home we're just not coming to see you again."

Spoken just like someone who had never slept one night away from her own bed, or her mother, in her entire life.

She didn't get it. How could they ever get it? My siblings looked so innocent sitting there. I felt like I was the wise big sister who already had more experiences than they could ever imagine.

I stared at each of them. God, I loved them so much. Josie wearing her plaid blazer, penny loafers and her perfect pompadour. Tony looking so young and handsome in his Eisenhower jacket and army boots. Paul looking very studious in his square glasses and open-collared white shirt. My brothers had each changed so much since I saw them last. Did any of them understand I had changed too, I wasn't the little sister who went away years earlier?

Paul and Josie held tightly to their packages for me, hoping whatever they contained would be just the thing to make me happy. A chair had been placed for me between them, so I sat down and savored the moment. Mother Superior was right, this certainly was a surprise. Tony was going overseas and he wanted to see me before he left. They couldn't refuse him. He smiled lovingly as he reached into his jacket and took out a comic book.

"I didn't have time to get you anything special" he said.

Special? He could never imagine how special anything from him was to me, even if it was something we were strictly forbidden to ever look at, like a comic book. But I certainly couldn't tell him that as I slowly slid it under the new coat my sister had brought me from home. It was a lovely camel coat with a dark brown velvet collar and cuffs, and I liked it very much. Paul brought me a new pair of brown shoes my mother had sent, and they fit perfectly.

They were each looking around the empty room, curiosity written all over their faces, so I told them what the room was used for and they appeared impressed. They were even more impressed when I told them we never went outdoors in the winter. I guess that was one of the many things they couldn't imagine about my life. We each looked a bit awkward as if we had never once lived together.

Paul finally asked Tony, "So, how does she look to you?"

"She's taller," he said, a bit sadly.

I wished their visit would never have to end, but before long Mother Superior was standing in the doorway and I knew it was over. They each hugged and kissed me as we said our good-byes and they promised to see me again soon. I asked Tony if he would be coming back too, and he said he didn't know because he was going very, very, far away. *Then he will know something about living with strangers too.* I turned away and didn't even wave as I followed Mother dry-eyed out of the room. I had been trained to contain my feelings in the presence of nuns.

The children were full of questions when I got back, and when I secretly showed them my comic book they were thrilled beyond words. After we had all quickly glanced through it, my anxiety of getting caught became too much for me, so several evenings later when Sister passed around the large bag for trash, I had already torn it up into a hundred pieces and dropped it into the bag. But I kept for myself the love each piece held for my brother so far away.

The following Saturday I had a "real" sin to confess to the new priest. I couldn't wait to tell him, and he was probably just as eager to hear it. Finally, there would be a break from the monotony of my usual three sins, two of which were actually lies. You see, I really did always tell the truth, and I certainly never talked after lights out. My only real sin was not finishing everything on my plate. Still, I had to tell him something every Saturday. Sometimes I would reverse the order of my sins, just to keep things interesting. But on that Saturday, I had a real sin, and I was very eager to see his reaction.

"Bless me Father for I have sinned. I looked at a comic book."

"Oh…and what did you do with that comic book, child?" he asked with a hint of shock.

"I tore it up and threw it away, Father."

"Ah now, that's my good girl! I want you to say three Hail Marys and three Our Fathers."

That's it? I mused to myself, that was hardly worth giving up my brother's precious gift for.

Just when I was convinced I had had all the visitors I would receive, there was yet another. A visitor, whose identity I will never know. Not ever.

One of the strictest rules at our house was no one was ever allowed out of bed after lights out. If you had to use the bathroom, wanted a drink of water or didn't feel well, you had to call Sister. One night I was awakened by the sound of the girl across the aisle from me calling for Sister in a very despairing tone. She was half crying half whining over and over again, "Sister Martha could you please come in here?"

This went on for several minutes without anyone else in the dorm making any kind of sound. I was very curious as to why the girls on each side of her didn't seem to hear her since I could. I lay there very still, waiting for the sound of Sister's padded steps to come running down the hall. But it never happened, and the girl's cries became louder and more fearful. Suddenly, in the moonlight coming in through the sides of the shades, I saw the outline of a figure come down the center aisle and turn right into the space between mine and Annie's bed, brushing along my covers.

Then I felt it, two firm taps on my right shoulder. My heart nearly exploded in my chest, blood felt like it was trying to gush out of my ears, making it impossible to hear if the figure was still standing over me or had moved away. My heart started to pound in a very unfamiliar rhythm. I thought I might be dying and didn't much care if I was. In sheer terror, I kept my eyes crushed closed, so I couldn't see where the figure was. Sweat started to trickle down my forehead and tickled my face. Yet I dared not move, I lay there paralyzed with fear, and I heard the crying girl say someone was sitting on her bed, but the rest of the room remained silent. And Sister never came.

I don't know how long it was before the girl stopped crying and everything was still again. I only know I never moved a single muscle until hours later, when daylight started sliding through the sides of the window shades. Slowly, and as casually as I could, I let myself roll over, and with eyes half-shut extended my aching arms and legs.

Gradually, I opened my eyes completely and saw everything looked like the start of any other day. The only difference was my mind was racing with questions. Why didn't anyone else hear what I heard? Who tapped me on my shoulder? These questions ruled out completely the possibility that the girl was just having a bad dream. Was it just one of the children sleepwalking? If so, why wouldn't the girl be eagerly telling everyone else in the dorm what she had experienced the night before? Instead, she chatted and laughed with the girls on both sides of her bed like nothing had occurred. The whole thing was maddening.

I decided to ask Annie, "Did you hear anything last night?"

"No, why, did you?" she replied a little too quickly, I thought.

"No," I said as casually as I could, convinced, for reasons unknown to me, it was the wisest thing to do.

Sister arrived after a while with her temperature cart and once again panic struck me. What if last night's experience caused me to spike a fever, and she tells me to stay in bed all day, which was her only remedy if one of us had a fever. That would mean being alone in the dorm all day. My mind almost couldn't handle that possibility. So, when she handed me the thermometer, I placed it between my teeth and cheek hoping that might lower the actual temperature. It must have worked, because she hesitated for a moment, then turned and placed it in the vial. My feeling of relief was unimaginable.

I continued to observe the girl for the remainder of the day. I watched her carefully at breakfast, in the classroom, at bedtime, for any sign of what might have happened the night before. But, she was her usual happy self, displaying virtually nothing to indicate the despair I had heard in the night. Yet I know what I heard that night, and more importantly, I know what I felt. What I don't know is who was walking around the dorm, who touched me, who frightened that child to tears, and why nothing reflected even a hint of what had happened. It was, and remains a mystery.

Days Remembered

*Let today embrace the past with remembrance,
and the future with longing.*

KAHIL GIBRAN, THE PROPHET

Over the course of almost three years there were, indeed, a number of other occurrences that still flash across my mind like the slides in an old projector. Some were humorous, others were not, and some were just lovely. There was the afternoon when Sister told us she was going to allow us to see a special event in the lives of the nuns called Vespers, which is a daily late afternoon church service. We were all excited as we obediently walked in line to the chapel. Inside, we sat up front on the left side of the center aisle, where we always sat on Sunday mornings, as we waited to see what would happen next.

In back of the chapel there stood a white pedestal, and on it were neatly stacked white veils. Not like bridal veils, but veils made of very fine cloth, thin enough to see through. As each nun entered the chapel, she lifted one of the veils from the pedestal, unfolded it and placed it over her head and face. Then she slowly walked down the aisle. The nuns softly sang hymns as they walked to their seats and sat widely spaced apart. The priest, wearing a thin white lacy top over his regular long black cassock, recited prayers in Latin at the altar and the nuns joined him at various intervals. It was all very lovely, and very impressive for young children to witness. The nuns looked and sounded so angelic, it gave me a lump in my throat as I stared intensely at them. Even Sister Martha looked angelic behind her veil, which was enough to convince me something purely divine was unfolding before our very eyes.

Outside, a summer rain fell softly on hot, thirsty, manicured lawns and flower beds.

Inside, we listened to raindrops tapping gently on the stained-glass windows overlooking the rows of nuns, creating a lovely background sound to their prayers and hymns. The scene seemed to be frozen in time, and I wanted nothing more than to be frozen in time with it. As we walked back afterward, I inhaled the lovely smell of wet soil in the flower beds surrounding us as I continued to contemplate what we had just witnessed.

My mind was definitely made up. When we got back to our building I took a vote. Sure enough, all the girls had decided to join the convent on their eighteenth birthday, just as I had. It would be wonderful to be part of the kind of ritual we had just observed every day, for the rest of our lives. Our unified resolve lasted for an entire week.

Ceremonial rituals can be very intoxicating. And no one can perform them better than Catholics. They add an important dimension to one's life that can last a lifetime. It was one of the reasons I loved being the official flower girl for the hospital — not only did it give me special status, but I was also part of beautiful ceremonies. I had my own special white dress and shoes for those occasions when two or more children were to receive their First Holy Communion, and for special Holy Days. I didn't wear a veil on those occasions, Sister made a beautiful wreath of fresh flowers to wear in my hair with a long, thin, satin streamer hanging behind it.

On Saturdays, before every ceremony, Sister and I went to chapel for rehearsal. I was shown how to walk and carry a small basket on my arm filled with flower petals to be dropped along the aisle as the Communion children followed behind me. The chapel was always filled with extra flowers on those special days, making it look even more lovely than usual. It was all very different from the memory of my own First Communion. But that day could never be compared to anything most children experience, and it held its own special beauty for me.

On one rehearsal Saturday, there was snow on the ground, and Sister told me to put on my heavy clothing because we were actually going to walk outside to the chapel. The children were beside themselves with envy, so I promised I would try to bring them back some real snow. We walked briskly to and from the chapel with Sister reminding me to hurry so I wouldn't get cold. Just outside our building on our way back, I saw my opportunity. I reached out to one of the bushes and grabbed a fistful of snow to hold in my pocket.

As we entered the building, we heard the phone ringing, and Sister told me to take off my coat and go directly to the playroom. The children circled around waiting for me to deliver on my promise. I pulled my hand out of my pocket, and opened it very slowly, only to find a tiny pool of water in the center of my palm. The children laughed so hard at my expense they were falling over themselves. But there was no way to convince them I really had held snow in my hand. When Sister returned, she wanted to know what all the laughing was about. We answered with one loud voice.

"Nothing, Sister Martha."

As I said, we got along amazingly well with each other, but we were still children, even if we were expected to behave like robots. Playtime in the playroom was when most of the skirmishes occurred, and Sister would come in and settle them promptly. Most of the time a girl would be caught right in the middle of doing something wrong, and the first words out of her mouth were, "Sister, I didn't do it!"

It was an exclamation I heard at least ten times a day, and Sister ignored it just as often. I promised myself if I was ever caught red-handed doing something wrong, I would never deny it. I lived to regret that promise.

Patty O'Malley was a problem waiting to happen. One day, Sister announced she was spending too much time in the laundry room washing underwear by hand because they were too soiled to be cleaned in the washing machine. And, if the situation didn't improve, we would have to wash them ourselves.

The following week, Sister announced she saw no improvement, so we would have a nightly panty crotch inspection. The girls found it hard to contain their laughter as we stood in line every night with panty crotches in hand, filing past Sister for inspection. I imagine it was the way she went about it that made it so hilarious — intense, serious and focused, like she was conducting the most important investigation in the world, when it was really only ridiculous.

The more we tried to contain our laughter, the more contagious it became, affording us far more enjoyment than embarrassment. And, of course, Patty started spending a lot of time in the evenings washing her panties in the bathroom sink. I would catch her elbow deep in soap suds and having a grand old time for herself. I often wondered if her panties were even dry by morning. I never inquired.

The underpants incident was the lighter of the Patty O'Malley calamities. Patty was different, and young children are not always understanding of differences. We tried to overlook a lot of her behavior, but one day she pushed us too far. The problem started with the way she began greeting each new day. Just before daybreak, Patty would rock back and forth on her bed, making her mattress springs squeak loudly. Her first finger pointed to the ceiling as she chanted, "Milkman, I have to go to the bathroom." She would repeat it over and over, until we were all awake before it was even light.

The rest of us racked our brains for ideas as to why she would be telling the milkman she had to go to the bathroom. Was it the clanking of milk bottles at that early hour that woke her? It didn't make any sense to any of us, and we felt compelled to put an end to it. We came up with the brilliant idea that whoever she woke up first would go over to her and yank one of her curls. We warned her beforehand about our plan, but it made no impression whatsoever, she just kept rocking and chanting.

One morning, as several of us were sitting up in bed in near darkness listening to her usual morning chant, I threw off my covers, marched right up to her and delivered the promised yank. I was followed by Rose, the co-author of our plan, then the other girls. Anna, whose bed was across the aisle from Patty's and was no doubt a future crusader, decided she was going to report our brutality.

Sister arrived on the scene looking pretty mean, mainly because it was Monday, which was laundry day for her and always put her in a foul mood. Patty whined as Anna eagerly filled Sister in on the details and the rest of us tried to interject how impossible it was to sleep with Patty's incessant chanting. The expression on Sister's face reflected both curiosity and empathy as she looked at Patty for a long moment, never questioning the absurdity of the child's behavior. I found that very puzzling. Didn't she think Patty's chanting at the crack of dawn to go to the bathroom was a bit strange?

After giving us a seething scolding, Sister decided we should get on with our morning activities in complete silence, and whoever finished making her bed first should go over and help someone else, so we could get things moving along quickly. Rose finished making up her bed first and immediately came over to help me, but not in silence.

Instead, she saw it as the perfect opportunity to tell me, "I hate that Anna banana, she's such a snitch."

The next thing I heard was Anna screeching, "Sister Martha! Mary D'Agostino just called me Anna banana!"

Sister appeared at the door again, this time with murder in her eyes. I looked up at Rose, who was still bending over my bed, looking completely terrified.

I couldn't do it. I couldn't say those utterly exhausted words, "Sister, I didn't say it!"

When I looked at Sister in the doorway, she was motioning for me to come forth with her famous index finger. I moved slowly down the aisle towards her. Just as I cleared the last bed a few feet in front of her, she reached out her arms towards me so far her sleeves pulled up almost to her elbows. Sister's ten fingers were spread wide like an eagle's claws as she gripped my hair, lifted me up, and put me down in front of her.

It went on for what seemed like an eternity, the shaking back and forth like a rag doll and lifting me up from the floor by my hair. All I could hear was her saying this would teach me not to call people names or hit anyone again. For a split second I thought, *She's really going to kill me.* What will they tell my mother?

When the thrashing finally stopped, she flung me to the floor against the front wall of the dorm and told me there would be no breakfast for me that morning. It was the best thing that had happened thus far that morning, until I remembered — it was a cold cereal morning.

The children filed past me as they left the dorm, and when I looked up through streaming tears, I saw Rose, whose shoulders were somewhere up around her ears as she looked down at me in silent guilt. I sat there for a very long time, feeling like my scalp had been torn from my head and trying to figure out how to get back into my family of sisters. I reasoned that whatever occurred was really my fault since I had encouraged the bullying along with the others. I decided I would tell Sister I was sorry.

When she finally appeared sometime before dinner, I simply said, "I'm sorry, Sister."

Well, one would have thought I had said something extraordinary the way she threw her arms around me and hugged me in her typical manic style. I almost wondered if Rose hadn't told her the truth in my absence, and my opinion of Rose was immediately temporarily heightened. Or perhaps Sister was feeling some guilt?

She rushed me into the playroom and announced, "Children, I want you all to know Mary has apologized for what she did. Isn't that just wonderful?"

Sister treated me afterwards as if nothing ever happened that day, and I treated Rose the same. As for Patty? She stopped calling out for someone to take her to the bathroom at the crack of dawn after that day.

Even after all these years, I still marvel at how twenty-five children were kept indoors all winter without any of the distractions children enjoy today. There was only one house we could see in the distance, and my assigned seat in the dining room had been changed to a spot where I could see it best. At every meal, I would stare at that house and wonder what the people who lived inside must be like. I pictured a real family, with a mother and father and, naturally, a little girl just about my age. They probably had a cat too, and their own car to go anywhere they wanted, like the movies or the circus. I fantasized about them endlessly.

On cold, gray, winter mornings, I would stare at the pencil-thin smoke rising from their chimney as it slowly zigzagged and sliced through a dark snow-threatening sky. I could picture how incredibly cozy it must be to live in that house. On Thursday evenings, after our cold suppers were over, Sister would ask who wanted to tell a story to entertain the children. I would sometimes raise my hand and tell a story from the images in my mind originating from that house. I told them about secret passages and ghosts if it was close to Halloween, or all manner of miracles and visions that happened to the family members if Easter was coming. And at Christmas, everyone got exactly what they asked for, but only after many obstacles were magically overcome.

In time, when Sister asked us who we wanted to tell a story, the others would shout, "Mary! Mary!"

It gave me enormous joy to hear that, and to realize my words had the power to hold people's attention. They even called me their best story-teller. And so, my love affair with words began.

Those long winter days were filled with lots of Sister's stories too. We sat cross-legged on the floor in the playroom, or at our desks in the classroom, while Sister spun one tale after another. Most of them were based on the lives of saints and the miracles they performed. Some of her stories would get a bit scary because they included visions of evil spirits. But she always reassured us afterward if we should ever see anything that frightened us, all we had to do was make the sign of the cross and we would be protected. Hearing that was very comforting, but I still found being alone in the dorms to be an extremely anxiety-inducing experience, especially after the night of the unknown visitor. I found myself thinking about my own guardian angel again and hoped she hadn't drifted off somewhere.

There were times when we had to be alone in the dorms for whole days at a time. When Sister took our temperatures in the morning, if there was even a hint of fever, she would say, "You need to stay in bed today." That meant complete bed rest.

It happened to me one morning after I woke from a nightmare about my Aunt Helen, who was my "other" mother. In my dream, she and I were happily walking along a street enjoying a beautiful day together. The sun was bright, making her straight jet-black hair shimmer and sparkle in the sunlight as it glided from side to side. Suddenly, she was hit by a yellow cab speeding around the corner and ended up lying dead in the middle of the street with me sobbing over her. When I awoke, my face was covered with sweat and tears, just as Sister was approaching my bed. I was confined to my bed for the next two days after that dream.

On those days, meals were brought to us on a tray. We ate alone and amused ourselves any way we could. I dreaded those days. I would color, play with a string, or cut paper dolls until the children returned for their naps. Even then, there was little time to talk and share. I'd have to wait until after supper, when they would tell me all the latest gossip about who got in trouble with Sister and who wasn't best friends with whom anymore, for whatever reason.

Sometimes, those lonely days were accompanied by bad weather. I'd stare out the windows, watching raindrops make rivulets that merged together and quickly made one thick stream that raced down the pane. I amused myself by trying to guess which stream would win. Those were also the days I thought about my family the most, always wondering what they were doing at that precise moment, attributing to them all of the emotional feelings they could be experiencing in my absence. There was only one feeling I tried not to imagine they could feel: relief. Yes, relief from my unrelenting fevers. Those early weekly Saturday morning clinic appointments at the hospital. The constant worrying about who would be available to take care of me. All those scary nosebleeds that left everything I wore stained down the front. The nine un-remembered months of being completely bedridden.

The city had provided my mother during those months a lady who came in daily to care for me. The woman was African-American and smiled a lot. I only recollect one day in her care, when she asked if I could manage to drink a cold glass of chocolate milk from a glass straw. Just as I finished, my mother walked in from work.

"Look Jenny, she finished this whole glass of milk."

My mother's face about split in half, her smile was so broad. I remember thinking, I wish I could make her smile like that at very meal, every day. But I couldn't.

Yes, I imagine my family felt more than a little relief. But I rarely allowed myself to think about that. Better to watch the raindrop races.

⌾⌾

If it's difficult to describe what the confinement of winter was like, it's just as hard to describe what the joy of going outdoors for the first time in spring was like. When Sister broke the news that we could actually go outside for a sustained amount of time, we were absolutely giddy. We raced down the back stairs to the play area, no command of "no running" was heard by anyone. The air had that indescribably sweet scent of new life emerging everywhere. Every twig of every tree had buds just ready to burst, and the ground was covered with green dots, not quite willing to give up the secret of their identity. I stretched out my arms, lifted my face up to the deep blue sky filled with cotton-ball clouds, and started to spin around and around, looking like some native Shaman performing an ancient ritual dance to the Sun God. It felt wonderful.

Far, far off in the distance, I heard a voice saying, "Now Mary D'Agostino you stop that spinning this minute before you fall."

But, I didn't stop, I was lost up there in those clouds, and I was free.

When I had my fill of that beautiful sky, Alicia and I dashed from one green spot to another, inspecting every sign of life and shouting over and over, "Look at this! And this!"

Sister Martha watched us like a mother hen, the breeze catching her veil just right and billowing it high around her shoulders, making her look like a large white bird guarding her flock. On days like that, she was very much caught up in our pleasure and it showed all over her face, making it hard not to love and trust her.

How could we not love and trust her to a certain degree? Sister, was all we had. To have done otherwise would have meant we had no mother figure at all, and that would have been far more painful for children so young, so far from their natural mothers. Consequently, we welcomed every bit of attention we could draw from her. To be allowed to even stand next to her when she read to us, and feel her hand stroke the back of our thighs as we leaned against her, was very special.

❦

During Sister's catechism lessons, she talked about the differences between mortal sin and venial sin. We never questioned why missing Mass for even one Sunday would result in burning in the fires of hell for all eternity if one should die before going to confession. Or why eating meat on Friday, also considered a mortal sin, should result in the same form of punishment. It sounded a bit harsh to me, but I dared not say so.

Venial sins, on the other hand, would condemn one to a place called purgatory, where you didn't burn in fire, but remained in a state of limbo for eternity. That didn't sound too good either, but it was certainly better than the alternative. Obviously, I decided it wise to remain in the venial sin category during my lifetime, even if I wasn't at all sure what sins those consisted of. As for heaven? Well, it sounded to me like only saints and angels went there, and we were all trying real hard to attain that status.

Still, Sister Martha was quite lovable at times. With special emphasis on "at times." She would occasionally come into the playroom and join us in a nursery rhyme circle dance, like "Farmer in the Dell," or play musical chairs with us. She would lift the edges of her skirt slightly and dance and play right along with us. How we cherished every second of those times.

Once, I remember being in her sewing room and seeing a rack of new dresses that had just arrived. I spotted a blue and white dotted Swiss dress and fell in love with it.

"Please, please, Sister, let me have this dress when you hand them out next Saturday morning, okay?"

"Only if you promise to eat everything on your plate until then." Her bargaining tool never changed.

The following week when she was placing dresses on our beds, there on my bed was the blue, dotted Swiss dress she knew I loved so much. Later that week, two other children and I were chosen to be in a picture with Mother

Mary Grace looking into a small goldfish pond. In the picture, I'm wearing that very dress.

However, there is another memory of that sewing room that showed the all-too-familiar, not very lovable side of Sister Martha.

One evening in the dorm, I had gotten into an argument with one of my sisters. Sister ended it by grabbing my hair and marching me into the dark sewing room. There were several metal lockers in the room, and she placed me into one of them. She almost shut the door completely before she reconsidered and returned to open it slightly. I imagine she remembered the pillow incident and didn't want to repeat it. She left the dark room and closed the door behind her. Through the slit of the locker door, I could see the moon shining through the bare branches of the tree outside the window. It was a cold, windy night, and the branches of the tree flapped wildly against the window pane, creating the most eerie sight and sound. I stood very still, so as not to add more frightening sounds to the howling winds and the flapping branches by rattling the metal locker too.

The voices of the children in the dorm had quieted down, and I knew it meant lights out.

I had started to panic thinking Sister might leave me there all night. When she entered the room, and opened the locker door, asking if I had learned my lesson, I quickly replied, "Yes, Sister," and she told me to go to bed without making a sound. When I pulled the covers over me that night, it was hours before I stopped trembling and finally fell asleep.

Like all children with their primary caregiver, we observed everything about Sister Martha. Like her spotless, white sneakers with deep cracks across the top from all the white, liquid polish she applied daily. The muslin cloth they were made of seemed to be molded to her feet, showing every joint of her toes and the bunions along the sides. We were very curious about her hair. What color was it? Was it long or short? One Saturday morning when she gave us our weekly bath and head wash, things got so hectic for her between the two bathrooms on opposite ends of the building, her headpiece became completely twisted around, allowing a clump of her hair to stick out. Well, that certainly answered our hair question. Her hair was short, partially gray, and looked as if it had just been randomly chopped off.

Another cause for our curiosity? Sister's room. The door of her room was next to the dining room, and one day as we were lined up before going in for dinner, we noticed it was ajar. We literally climbed over each other to get a glimpse inside. The room was incredibly small and colorless, consisting of what appeared to be a small cot neatly made up against one wall, an end table and a small wooden chair. To call its contents sparse would be a huge understatement. We couldn't see the other side of the room behind the door, but we assumed there must have been a bathroom there, because she never used ours. At least not that we ever observed.

Everything about Sister's life seemed shrouded in mystery, and we were always trying to fill in the gaps. She never talked about her family, or even where she came from. It was almost as if she had dropped out of the sky and into a life consisting only of us. And no amount of prompting ever revealed anything else. We knew she ate at least one meal with the other nuns. That I had discovered on my seventh birthday with the birthday cake fiasco. Otherwise, Sister Martha remained somewhat of a mysterious figure without any clues to go by.

Since we knew nothing of the outside world, or what kind of restrictions the war was inflicting on the general population, Sister's walking through the halls at night, or entering the dorms carrying a gaslight lantern, only added to her aura of mystery. On those evenings, her image would slide up the walls, casting huge scary shadows all the way down the narrow halls, and the glow of the gaslight she carried made her figure in white appear ghostly. It was enough to make us think hard before we called her for anything. She was probably just abiding by the blackout rules due to the war, but since non-disclosure was the order of the day, we filled in the gaps of our knowledge with our own childish imaginings, which most of the time were wrong.

Even very young children know when they have passed through one stage and entered a whole new place in their world. For me, it came on a cold visiting Sunday, probably in the late months of my second year. Outside, small snow flurries darted around in every direction, the way they do when a serious snowstorm is on its way. I watched them calmly from my seat in the auditorium, waiting for my mother, and perhaps even my sister, to appear at the door. There was not a great deal of excitement inside me that day. Something had changed.

The other children sat patiently in their seats, and the nuns milled around with their hands folded behind the front panel of their habits. I loved the way they looked when they did that, so calm and serene, even angelic.

As the welcome nun at the door started to take the names of the first visitors, I had this vague feeling we were almost being invaded. I had come to like the cloistered existence we all shared without even realizing it. It ceased to matter if anyone came to visit or not.

My mother came alone that day, filled with loving tenderness and bearing all sorts of gifts. I could feel the coldness coming off her clothing as we hugged and kissed, the sensation so foreign to me. Her visit that day, as always, was a good visit. My mother filled me in on all the news from home, which was mostly about how my young cousins were doing, and whether Timmy still remembered me. He seemed to be quite a handful for my Aunt, and my mother filled me in on every little piece of mischief he got into. The memory of my little cousin had faded, I couldn't even remember that little boy smell he had after playing in the dirt on hot summer days. As for his baby sister, Jeana, who by then was two-and-a-half years old, I had nothing to forget. My mother seemed to love the fact that she looked a little Asian, and she undoubtedly enjoyed her more. I didn't even feel a little jealous of the fact she had another baby to love. I was far beyond that, and followed each detail with, "Tell me more, Mommy, tell me more."

I had long since stopped asking why some members of the family had never come to visit. It seemed like a moot point, and we both knew it.

I remember feeling a bit restless during her visit that particular Sunday, without a clue as to why. Before I knew it, the visit was over. Visitors started heading towards the door, and as usual, my mother was the last to get up. When she did, we hugged and kissed as always, and she continued to throw me kisses after she left her seat. She slid along the wall behind a sea of mothers and fathers, which seemed to swallow her up as they slowly moved towards the door.

It never seemed unusual to see my mother as a single person because that was the way it had always been. I never saw my parents relating to one another in any kind of loving way like my peers did, although it would have been nice, and I even fantasized about it at times. But my mother was facing life alone, without the comfort of a mate to share life's burdens. Unlike the other less pretty women around her who clung to their husbands, she clung only to her purse. For the first time that day, I saw her as vulnerable, and it saddened me to think of her making that long trip home alone. I wondered what she thought about on those trips. Still, I found myself wishing she would hurry up and leave so I could find out what gifts my sisters had gotten.

As I waved good-bye to her for the last time that day, all I could think about was what we might be having for supper that evening. I was thinking, Maybe, we'll have baked macaroni and cheese. I'll ask Sister to give me the burnt crispy part. I knew she'd give me anything I wanted if it got me to eat.

I had crossed over. I was completely institutionalized. On a very deep level I was prepared to remain in All Saints Hospital for the rest of my life. The people there had become my family.

IX

The Stranger Within

*You need to claim the events of your life,
to make your life real.*

Anne-Wilson Schaef

Aliciaand I had remained best friends for most of two-and-a-half years. While that may not exactly be "forever," it was a very long time in the lives of children. Each of us had started to include more of the other girls in our play as we grew older. The girl who still slept in the bed next to me was Annie, and she became my closest friend for the remainder of my days there. What I remember most about Annie was her calmness, her easy manner. It seemed to come from someplace deep inside her. Sometimes she almost appeared to have a precious secret only she knew. I wanted to be more like her than anyone else.

One afternoon at nap time, Annie suggested we reach out to each other across the small space between our beds and just gently glide the tips of our fingers back and forth on each other's hand while spelling out a word or numbers to be guessed. She offered to take the first turn. I extended my hand to her, and she gently allowed the tips of her fingers to go back and forth along the back of my hand. At first it was only ticklish, but it became extremely soothing.

"Now it's my turn," she whispered.

I imitated her motions exactly, and then it was my turn again. We went back and forth only a few more times before an extraordinary thing happened. For the first time since I arrived years ago, I fell asleep during naptime.

When Sister arrived with her temperature cart, I was just waking up. I looked over at Annie and asked, "What happened?"

"You fell asleep, and just when it was my turn too," she said, laughingly.

"Wow! I haven't fallen asleep at naptime since I came here."

"Really?"

"Never, not even in the other dorm."

"Wasn't that fun, and didn't it feel nice?"

"Oh yes, let's do the same thing tomorrow too."

"Okay."

As we continued to do it, I fell asleep again and again, marking yet another turning point of my confinement.

After about a week, I woke up one day to a dark, empty dorm. I jumped out of bed and ran screaming down the hall. Sister came out of the playroom and caught me midway.

"What's the matter?" she said gently.

"Why didn't you wake me up like you always do with the other girls? How could you just leave me in the dark dorm?" I yelled accusingly.

"Because you need your sleep, Mary, that's why." she answered calmly, which was very unusual for Sister.

We both walked back to the dorm and she waited for me to dress and fix my bed without saying another word. I was puzzled by Sister's behavior, and furious with Annie for not waking me up. When I caught up with her later in the playroom, I lashed out at her.

"Annie how could you do that to me? Why didn't you wake me up? And how did everybody get dressed, make up their beds, and leave without me hearing anything?"

"Because," she protested, "Sister was holding her finger across her lips, you know how she always does, and saying, 'Shhh,' when she saw you sleeping. She wouldn't let anyone talk the whole time she took temperatures. And even after, when we were getting dressed. That's why!"

Why would she do that? I wondered. She never did it to anyone else when naptime was over, she would poke their nose with the wet thermometer to make sure they woke up. Why this sudden concern for my sleep? Did she notice something about me?

"You have to promise me Annie, if the same thing happens tomorrow, you'll wake me up, you have to promise me that," I demanded.

"But I can't, I'll get in trouble if I wake you up."

"Not if you do it accidentally on purpose you won't."

"And how am I supposed to do that?"

"When you're making up your bed tomorrow and you come around to my side, just accidentally on purpose let your hip hit my bed. That will be enough to wake me up, and she'll never know. I would do it for you Annie. You know I would."

"Okay, but if I get in trouble..."

"You won't, don't worry. And I'll take the blame if she ever finds out."

The next day I was awakened by the gentlest nudge against my bed, and Annie was looking ever so innocent. I sat straight up so Sister would see I was awake and come back with her cart, while I simultaneously gave Annie a knowing wink. I loved her more that day than ever, because she not only put me to sleep, she made it safe for me to fall asleep.

A couple more weeks went by, and it was again time to be seen by Dr. Tara and the others at the hospital building. When the angry-looking lady doctor finished listening to my heart, I noticed she put my binder on a different shelf from the others in my building, but I erased the act from my mind immediately. Then it was time to be weighed, and I had actually gained over one pound. Sister was thoroughly delighted and proud, like she had finally succeeded.

While we were in class several mornings later, the door opened and Sister walked up to the teacher and asked that I be excused for a few minutes. When I walked out in the hall with her she dug down into her deep side pocket and handed me a small bottle to fill with urine. My heart almost leaped out of my chest, but I told myself it was only a coincidence. Still, in the toilet stall, I was shaking so bad I peed all over my hand, and it was almost impossible to retrieve enough urine to fill even half the bottle. That should have been a clue that something was going on inside me, but at that age we really don't recognize the face of denial. Later, all the girls were convinced I was being made ready to go home.

In the days that followed, I watched Sister every moment she was in our presence for some clue in her demeanor towards me. Nothing changed. After several more days went by, I started to settle back into the routine of our days, satisfied that I had been right all along.

I don't know why we didn't go to class that day, but we were sent straight to the playroom instead, which was a happy change. We all had our favorite games, mine was playing ball and jacks, and I immediately found some partners. I had become one of the best players in our group. I could actually lift one jack off another without moving the first one, and all the girls loved to challenge me.

We were in the middle of a really good game that morning after breakfast, when the door of the playroom opened and Sister tapped the upper glass portion with her ring as usual for silence. All of us immediately stopped playing to hear what she had to say.

"Girls I want you all to say goodbye to Mary D'Agostino because she will be leaving us to go home today."

I dropped the ball, my heart and my identity all in the same instant. Only the sound of my sisters' unanimous cry of "Oh no!" was louder than the sound of my heart.

They rushed around me from all sides, reaching out to grab me while Sister pressed through them to put her arm tightly around my numb body and whisk me out the door, just as she had done the first day I arrived. I heard the door close behind me, and the knocking of the children's knuckles against it.

I felt something inside me split and didn't recognize the person who emerged. It was like being out of my body and floating above, watching this child wrap her arms around Sister's waist, yelling, "No, no, I don't want to go! Please, please, just let me stay here!"

Who was this child? She couldn't be me. Hadn't I waited and prayed for this moment for almost three years? What is she talking about?

Again, Sister had to half drag me to the sewing room where she would change me into my own clothes sitting on the top shelf. When we got there, I pulled at her dress in every direction in an effort to keep her from reaching for that brown shopping bag. It was a surreal scene, me sobbing and begging to stay with her and the children. The whole world had suddenly gone mad in an instant.

"But Mary, you are all better now, and you can finally go home and be with your Mother. Isn't that wonderful?" she reasoned.

"No, I don't want to! I changed my mind! I want to stay with you. Please, please, Sister, just let me stay," I sobbed.

Contrary to her usual behavior, Sister remained calm and loving as she gently undressed me and put on my own clothes, which were wrinkled and small. My arms hung out from the sweater sleeves inches above my wrists, the dress was high above my knees — I looked ridiculous.

"Look how stupid I look," I wailed.

"No! No! Look how much you've grown!" she said excitedly.

When I looked down at her as she tied my shoes, her eyelashes were dark and heavy with tears. I was stunned how human and vulnerable she looked.

"You don't even love me, you never loved me!" I shouted accusingly.

"That is not true, Mary, I love you very much. I have always loved you."

Her voice was low, almost whispering, as she slid her forearm across her eyes just like a child might do, and stood up. With that simple motion of brushing away her tears, our relationship was healed forever.

"We must hurry now Mary, Mother Superior will be here soon with your brother, Paul, who will be taking you home today."

She was back in control. She had only allowed herself perhaps a few moments to be fully human. No more.

"What? Where is my mother?" I demanded.

How much more could I take in? I suddenly decided I didn't even like my brother. Why would my mother do this to me?

"Your mother didn't feel well, so she sent your brother instead. Now, who is your best friend so I can get her to help you empty out your cabinet?"

She said it all in one breath as she straightened her headpiece, which was almost completely undone by then from all my pulling. I saw more of her chopped up hair that day than the other children would probably ever see, and I wished I could tell them what it looked like.

"I have two best friends, Alicia and Annie, and I want them both," I said firmly.

"No, the rule is you can only pick one girl to help you."

Rules, of course. Even at a time like that, the rules must never be broken. I was too heart-sick to argue. I knew Alicia would be crushed. Hadn't we promised to be friends forever? Yet, it was Annie who was probably more responsible than anyone else for my going home, because she put me to sleep every afternoon.

"I guess it's Annie then," I whispered.

"Good, then I'll be right back."

When they returned, Annie looked so sad and pale it was unbearable to look at her. The three of us walked back to the dorm, and I opened my cabinet door, noticing for the last time the replaced hinge that had once given me so much grief. Slowly, I pulled out my belongings, and we placed them into the two shopping bags Sister had provided, with a reminder that I would not be able to fit too much into them.

Whenever I came across something I thought Annie might like, I asked her, "Would you like this, Annie?"

Her response was always the same, only a sad nod of her head. When we finished, the three of us walked slowly out of the dorm, and I never looked back.

As we turned to go down the center hall, I saw Mother Superior standing against the molding of the door of the playroom, each of her hands tucked into the sleeve of the opposite arm as she smiled sweetly. The faces of the children were still pressed against the glass where I left them, just quietly watching. Paul was standing on the top step of the short stairwell that led out of the building. As we approached him, I could see the look of bewilderment on my poor brother's face. He had undoubtedly thought he would be the hero of the day, rescuing me from the place I had so much wanted to leave, taking me home again. How could he have known he was taking me away from what had become my home?

As I approached Mother Superior, I knew exactly what she was thinking as she took my face between her hands.

"Do you remember that day, long ago, when I said you would cry just as hard on the day you left us as you did on the day you came, Mary? Now, I guess you believe me."

She hugged me warmly, and I turned again to Sister, who had just remembered my sink was still in the playhouse.

"We will have to send it to you later, your brother can't possibly carry that too."

I assured her I didn't want to take the sink away from the playhouse and that leaving it behind was my way of giving the other children something to remember me by. She thought that was a wonderful idea, and she promised she and the children would never forget me as she hugged me tightly for the last time. I couldn't embrace Annie like I wanted, her lips were quivering too much, and she was so pale. I just mouthed the words "good bye," and she did the same. As I clutched the small tan teddy bear that didn't fit in the shopping bag, my brother and I walked down the several steps to the front door, to leave St. Michael's forever.

When the door closed behind us, I looked up and saw the Yellow cab waiting. This time, it was faced in the opposite direction.

The driver jumped out of the cab to relieve my brother of the two shopping bags and put them in the trunk. Paul had to help me into the back seat, because I was doubled over, sobbing. When he slipped in on his side of the cab, he kept looking out the rear window.

"Mary, the children are all waving at the windows, you have to at least wave back to them before we leave."

He gently took my arm at the elbow, and I turned so he could wave my limp arm back and forth for them. The children were waving wildly and tapping on the pane. Sister stood in the background, not waving, just a figure in white staring straight ahead.

I heard the crunching of pebbles beneath the wheels, and it seemed everything was happening in reverse of that first day. The driver kept looking in his rear-view mirror, watching us without saying anything. There was a slight bump under the wheels as the cab turned right, and we were on the paved road heading away from the home I had known for so long.

"How long was she in that place?" the driver finally found the courage to ask.

"Thirty-two months," my brother answered without a moment's hesitation.

"Wow, that's a long time. No wonder she's taking it so hard."

"Yeah, I know."

He had counted every single month? was all I could think. What a testimony of love he had conveyed to me without his even realizing it. I suddenly remembered I did love him very much, even if I still wanted to be going home with my mother that day.

When we boarded the train, the two of us must have made a curious sight. A young man holding two bulging shopping bags, and a little girl with clothes that were far too small for her body, sobbing relentlessly. I could feel my brother's embarrassment, but the pain inside was far too much to contain.

He finally leaned over at some point and said ever so softly in my ear, "Mary, could you please try to stop crying, people are staring at us."

"I know, I'm trying, I just can't make myself stop."

I looked out the window in an effort to steer my thoughts away from Sister and the girls. I watched the trees gradually surrender to small homes, which then became less and less until they too surrendered to tall buildings. The train passed through tunnels that were dark and scary before it entered the station in New York City, where we transferred to yet another train that would take us to Brooklyn.

Everywhere I looked people all seemed to know exactly where they were going and were trying to get there in the fastest way possible. This pace of life was totally foreign to me, coming from the tranquil and serene environment I'd known for so long. It felt like I was moving around on another planet. A planet that was pretty dirty, I might add.

As I gazed out the windows of the train I could see mothers strolling along dirty, narrow streets, pushing baby carriages or running after toddlers. Some people sat on their front stoops or half hung out of their apartment windows, passively watching life go by. Women were hanging their clothes out to dry, their sheets all puffed up and billowing from the wind, reminding me how Sister Martha's veil looked when the breeze caught it. I saw their clotheslines zigzagging back and forth between windows of narrow courtyards. I noticed small flags hanging in almost every window. Some had one star, some had two, and some even had three. I finally turned to Paul and asked why were there so many flags hanging in windows. He said they represented someone in the family who was away fighting the war. There was so much I didn't know about this world I had left behind.

After a while Paul turned to me and said, "We're almost home, Mary."

My heart raced in my chest with anticipation. I tried to ignore the ugly streets below the elevated train we were riding, which groaned and squeaked loudly as it turned the corners of the track. There were hardly any trees on those streets, just some dry leaves that swirled in circles, rushing towards the curbs and under parked cars. I think that was the first day I fully realized there was a very ugly side to being poor. There was no beauty to be found anywhere, but what did it matter? I was going home, and that was where real beauty awaited me.

When Paul and I descended the stairs of the elevated platform, I looked around hoping to see something familiar. Most of what I saw looked foreign to me, except the sidewalks. They were mostly made of dark gray slate slabs, some crooked and uneven, others straight and level. We walked several blocks before I spotted the corner grocery store we lived above, and I remembered.

When we reached the building, I looked up and saw a flag in our window with one star on it for my brother, Tony. We climbed up the few stone steps of our stoop and stood in front of the old double door with narrow, oval glass panels. We stepped inside a tiny vestibule with a floor made up of small, octagonal black and white tiles. On the right wall, I saw our name on the mailbox. There was a second half-glass door to enter before the main hall, and when we opened that door, it was almost pitch-black inside. Sunbeams followed behind us, lighting up small dust particles dancing in the air, and allowing enough light that I could just about make out the stairwell.

My mother was looking down at us from the second-floor landing, asking my brother if we had made the trip all right. He assured her we had no problems as the two of us climbed the steps. When we reached the landing, she had more questions for him, asking whether he had made sure we hadn't forgotten any of my toys. He told her we had to leave the sink behind, which upset her. That's when I jumped in, telling her I wanted to leave it for the children, so they wouldn't forget me.

"Oh, you wanted to leave it? Then it's okay," she said.

Her face showed clear lines of stress, and she looked pale and tired. She wore a floral print housedress with buttons down the front and deep pockets. The dress had obviously seen too many washings, because the edges of the flowers were faded and melted into each other, creating almost a rainbow of circles. Her normally beautiful, thick, dark brown hair looked limp and lifeless. Her large almond-shaped eyes were filled with apprehension and fear. I could sense the anxiety and doubt she was feeling, but was unable to give her the assurance she needed, that I was completely recovered and safe now to love.

☙❧

The half-glass opaque door to the apartment was open, and I slowly moved towards it. When I stepped inside, I was shocked, the whole kitchen appeared shrunken. It was clean, but pitifully poor looking. Everything remained exactly as it was when I left — the worn linoleum in front of the big ugly stove, the sink attached to the wall, which stood on two front legs. Next to the sink sat an empty dish rack on the cover of a wash tub. The flooring had pulled away from the moulding, curling slightly upward and leaving an ugly empty space. A cafe curtain hung on the one window, slightly concealing the fire escape. It sagged a bit in the middle because, instead of a curtain rod, it hung from a rope-like binding material my mother used to make her lampshades. Over the small kitchen table pushed up against the wall hung a shelf with a tiny radio on it. The radio was playing, and someone was singing "I'll Be Seeing You."

I was standing in the middle of the room, taking everything in, when I realized my mother and brother were standing behind me. I wished I could have caught his words in mid-air before they reached my ears.

"Don't you think you should at least kiss the kid after she's been gone for almost three years?"

His words explained away the lack of "natural order of things" I was experiencing deep inside but would never have allowed to surface.

My mother then engulfed me in her arms saying, "Oh, of course, my bella mamma," as she smothered me with kisses.

An invisible wall went up between us that both frightened and protected me at the same time. Disenchantment spilled over me like a cold winter rain. Why did he need to tell her?

My homecoming apparently was ill-timed. My mother needed surgery, so again, she would be faced with the dilemma of who would be available to care for me while she was in the hospital, and perhaps even afterwards. Had I known that at the time, it might have explained her angst at the prospect of once again being responsible for a child she had become completely adjusted to not having to care for. But could there have ever been a "better time" for my homecoming? I wondered about that.

Paul didn't stay long. He kissed me goodbye and promised to see me again real soon and teach me how to tell time by myself. In his eyes, I saw the realization that things between us would be very different in the future because of the hours we had just shared. My thoughts then went to the next most important person in my life, and I wondered what kind of a greeting she would have for me.

"Mommy, where is Josie? When will she be coming home?"

"Josie has a job now, but she'll be home in a couple of hours."

"Where is Susie? I want to see her."

"Oh, your doll? Yes, yes of course, she is right on your little armchair. Do you remember the chair I had re-covered for you just before you went away? I made sure no one ever touched your doll while you were gone."

No doubt she was referring to my little cousins, whom I was also very anxious to see. I walked into the front room where the little chair sat below the window. I opened the much-dreamed-about case and picked up my little Susie. I held her in my arms with all the love of a returning mother. Unfortunately, she seemed far too small and inadequate to fill the massive hole I had in my heart for the children and nun I had just left behind. I went to the sink and filled her little bottle with water so I could test her wetting feature. Outside, the sounds of the street startled me. Cars honked their horns, children yelled back and forth, and ladies' heels made clicking sounds on the slate sidewalks. These had all become foreign sounds, long forgotten.

My mother watched me closely as I cradled Susie in my arms. She looked lost for words, so she said the only words she seemed to know, "Are you hungry? What would you like me to cook for you?"

"Could I have French fries with ketchup?"

"Of course you can, I'll make as many as you want."

Once, those words would have made me so happy, but that day they were empty as I thought of my sisters who were probably eating prunes just about that time.

I heard someone coming up the stairs, and my heart leaped with delight when I saw my sister Josie opening the kitchen door. I hung back, standing behind one of our kitchen chairs, as I awaited her reaction. She rushed into the room with open arms and crushed me with hugs.

"You're home! You're home!" she kept repeating.

And I remembered how much I loved her.

My mother had decided baby lamb chops might go well with the French fries, so she broiled some on a wire grilling rack she held over the open flame of the ugly stove. The aroma of the burning fat along their edges was incredible. Then, with Susie on my lap, the three of us sat down for supper exactly as I dreamed we would someday. Soon both of them were deep in conversation. I quietly dipped each French fry into the ketchup on my plate, allowing my taste buds to re-acquaint themselves with the tangy taste. I found it enjoyable to hear my mother intersperse Italian words in just the right places of her conversation, emphasizing whatever point she was trying to make. I had forgotten how she always did that. I had forgotten a lot of things.

Now and then my sister interrupted their conversation with a comment such as, "She's gotten so quiet, Ma."

Like I wasn't even there.

It's a funny a thing about coming home: Things can look the same, even smell the same, but something is different. It was me. I was different. Neither of them seemed to realize I had been away from them for far too long. Many bonds had been created, many struggles had been overcome without their help, or even their knowledge. I had released my old life with them. The little person who sat with them that evening could never be the same little person who left. I had been through a rite of passage, and had survived.

That night I slept in the big bed, squashed between my mother and sister. Although I had been put to bed hours earlier, I lay awake long after I heard them breathing heavily in sleep. I took long deep breaths through my nose, smelling the traces of lamb chops that still hung in the air and the scent of my sister's cologne on the sheets. I was back with the people I was born to, and it was all in the natural order of things. Those earlier concerns of the day, that my little sisters would soon forget me, had turned around completely. Instead, I hoped Annie would forget me quickly and instantly fall in love with the new girl who would occupy my bed by the next day. I didn't want her or Alicia to be feeling what I felt.

I heard it before I smelled it: Bloop, bloop, bloop...Coffee! My brain flooded with nerve endings greeting that all-too-familiar aroma. What an improvement over the smell of rubbing alcohol at the end of a wet thermometer. I thought of the children back at the hospital.

When I rolled over in bed, my sister was sitting in front of the dresser mirror redoing her pompadour over and over again. Each time it looked exactly the same as the last, but she seemed to not be satisfied. As I observed her, I wondered if I would still be the center of her universe. I had serious doubts, since that morning it appeared the center of her universe was herself. When she went into the kitchen for breakfast, my mother and her immediately melted into conversation that included intermittent low whispers when they spoke of me. As I listened, they seemed to fill each other so completely. A single mother and an adult daughter. Theirs was a bond that could never be broken, or even interrupted. I realized neither of them needed me as much I needed the family I left the day before.

I waited until Josie left for work, then I went into the kitchen. My mother was eager for me to eat a soft-boiled egg for breakfast. It would not have been my first choice, but I said not a word. I would have eaten the leg off the chair if that was what she wanted. There would never again be any opposition about food in her kitchen from me. She watched me intently as I polished off everything on my plate and the cup of milk with a bit of coffee in it.

Finally, she spoke. "Were you dreaming of the nun last night?"

"Nun? No Mommy, I didn't dream about anything. Why?"

"Well, you were calling her in your sleep last night, saying, 'Sister Martha I have to go to the bathroom,' over and over again, even after I tried to wake you."

Her eyes held confusion, and more than a little bit of sadness. "You know, you have to forget that nun."

"Her name is Sister Martha."

"Yes, I know. But I'm your real mother, not her. Whatever it is you want, just ask me and I'll get it for you."

"Oh Mommy, I know that! But I was sleeping, I didn't even know I was calling her."

I imagine my mother had finally started to understand I had been away from her far too long. Her eyes looked at me searchingly, and it became very hard to swallow. I watched her as she went to the sink and quietly started to wash the dishes in the same faded housedress she had worn the day before. Slowly and absently, she placed each dish neatly on the rack. Her head was leaning to one side in a kind of defeated and resigned way. Maybe she was sad, wondering if someone had usurped my love for her during that long absence.

The kitchen was incredibly drafty, making the floor feel like an ice rink, so I sat with my knees drawn up close to my body and wrapped my arms around them. Sister would have said this was very unladylike. It made me smile to think of that. Only the soft music Josie left playing on the small radio broke the silence as my thoughts slid back to the day before. Could it be? Was that what it's all been about? I asked myself. Love?

First, I thought of Sister Martha's announcement of my leaving. How she never defended herself against my outbursts of rage. Nor did she even try to resist my tearing her veil off her head and the wimple beneath it. She just continued to gently remove my hospital clothes and dress me in my own. Then her tears as she laced up my shoes. She was crying, I saw her myself. She had said, "I've always loved you."

Had she come to love me in spite of herself? Did she forget the vow of detachment of her non-secular community? Did Mother Superior with tear-filled eyes also forget how to appear calm and composed at all times, as she did that first day? Images of the last day were bringing up all sorts of questions. And the only answer? They had all done the best they could. All of them, my mother especially, were demonstrating in their own, perhaps flawed way that they loved me and had even managed somehow to save my life.

It was all so very confusing, this love thing. How could it hurt so much at times? Were there different kinds of love? Did some kinds of love leave and return again? Were there other kinds of love that lasted a lifetime, and still others that could be murdered in an instant? The questions seemed endless, and thinking about them was making my head hurt. I remembered Susie and realized the day that stretched out before me was long and languid, free of rules or rhythm.

The sun spilled through our front room windows, warming the floor beneath my bare feet and chasing away all the drafts. Outside, the neighborhood was waking up. Cars honked, people chatted, lady's heels clicked on the sidewalks and toddlers cried. This was the real world again — dirty, smelly, loud and complicated. It was the first of many days I could have to just play all day if I wanted, and those were the thoughts I entertained. Tomorrow I would let myself think about the children and her again. None of them would ever go away, they would live inside me forever.

I picked up the doll and felt warm and complete inside. Everything seemed to fit, and there was no need to search for answers anymore. I felt almost assured mine would be a perfect life from then on because I had survived such an ordeal. What could I really know about life except for what was seen through the eyes of a very young child's view of her most recent experience? But for that moment, a vaguely familiar feeling was stirring inside me. Hard to recognize at first, but then I remembered. It was very akin to — how should I say it — joy perhaps? But, on that day and in that particular time and place. Yes, indeed, joy would be accurate.

Epilogue

Sometimes, even now in the winter of my life, when I hear the swooshing sound of a brisk breeze rustling through the trees on my morning walks, I can almost hear their voices.

"Sister Martha, are you going to play Treasure Hunt with us today, are you, are you?"

"Yes, my little chicks."

"Yippee! Yippee!"

"I'm first!"

"Oh Sister, she always wants to be first, she's such a big baby."

"I am not! You are!"

"Now, now, children, we'll have none of that. Come, all of you and gather around me under our big tree, I promise everyone will get her chance."

The breeze passes, the leaves are still again and I remember, they are in the winter of their lives too. Oh

God, how I hope life has been good to them. Maybe I will see them again.

If I could, I would say, "You know I wrote a book about our years there together."

To which they would surely answer, "But Mary, now it's not 'your' story anymore, you gave it away."

"Yes, I did, it doesn't belong to me anymore, it can have a life of its own now. Maybe even be helpful and enjoyed by others, and isn't that wonderful!"

About the Author

Mary D'Agostino was born and raised in Brooklyn, NY. In 1985, she received her BA from Adelphi University in Garden City, NY. After relocating to SC, she taught Creative Writing at USC of Beaufort, SC, and has since written a number of published articles on human interests and social issues. She now lives in NC with her husband Duane Fuller. *Invisible Imprints* is her first book. For more writings, visit maryimprints.com.

53667993R00126

Made in the USA
Columbia, SC
19 March 2019